Memories of the Blue Door

Memories of the Blue Door

A true story by
Neil Davis and Paul Durkin

First published in 2012 by
Lifeguard Tower 19 Productions
www.tower19productions.co.uk

A CIP catalogue record for this book is available from the British Library

ISBN 978–0–9571514–0–6

Lovingly created by Infinite Authors
Printed in Great Britain by Berforts Group, Hastings and Stevenage

Contents

Acknowledgements

A thank you...

27years in the making, and still a desert load of sand left standing in the hour glass. They said a friendship ain't there forever? I knew of one that lasts!

A thank you to the friends who have always known me, with out them it's impossible to grow.

Thanking Mr Durkin, who never tires of my ideas, my fears, even after all these years.

A thank you to my dear loving mother, the one who had me, the best any son could know.

A thank you to my Father, for your energy, for your humour.
I thank my sister... always felt honoured to have grown up with you. As time screams on by, how I miss you.

A thank you to my three nieces, I watched you all stumble to walk, mumble to talk. and grow up with individual minds and an undoubted beauty all of your own.

A thank you goes out to my boy, my one and only boy, my universal pride and joy!

Finally a thank you to my blue eyed girl...without her there is no world. Chaos in socks? My world she truly rocks.

Your two boys are so lucky to have and know you young Edney!
And a big thank you to you my friends if you bought this book, for the chance you just took... Even if you own the only ever copy, because of you, it seems we did after all this time, really sell a book!
Neil

Just a quick acknowledgement to say thank you to my friends and family who believed in this book and especially the Blue Door Lads. Without you, this never would have happened!

Friendship never dies.

Flappy x
(Paul)

Foreword

In 1984, friendship was free and abundant. You and a pal could travel to the ends of the world and back without a care or a penny to share.

For nine little souls who needed nothing but one another, we had that dream. Long before Play Stations and Disneyland, we had it all and better within ourselves, within our minds.

Around the big Blue Door you would find us each and every night. Through the eyes of children, we return once again.

This is a tale about the greatest friends we ever had, a story without an end.

Like we said… in 1984, friendship cost you nothing.

I may speak for a lot of people when I say that their school days were the best of their lives. Not necessarily going to school (who liked that?), but the friends you made and the adventures you had during your youth. Unless you have plenty of money or are so laid back you're nearly lying down, there is probably not a more carefree and stress-free time of your life. Sure, you're thinking about GCSEs and maybe the prospect of work when you finish the 5th year, (or year 12 as it's now called), but that's a million miles away from mortgages, car insurance, loans, credit cards and being married with children.

I also think the youth of today have it easy. I don't want to sound condescending or pretend I'm a 95-year old fuddy-duddy, but my idea of entertainment and adventure at the age of thirteen, compared to that of today's kids, was very different. I know what you're thinking – things change, move with the times, you miserable sod, but from the experience of having my own children, I know my son would be mortified if I confiscated his X-Box, Play Station, Wii, (delete where applicable), and told him to go climbing trees, build dens or have a game of World Cup singles on the local piece of derelict land. Whatever happened to conversation? E-mails and mobile phone text messages make it easier for communication, but the art of dialogue has been lost in the super-highway of technology. I agree that with time comes change, but I think the culture shift has been massive over the last ten years or so. My friends and I often hung around in groups of eight or more, as teenagers do these days. The difference is, we never caused bother or harassed anyone, (there may be a small white lie in there somewhere!), and we were never served ASBOs like the chav culture of today. Put up your hand up if you feel intimidated by the Burberry cap, Rockport boots and the Borghoose jacket, (Berghaus to the people from Ponteland). Phrases like, 'Here, mister, can ya lend us a snout?' or, 'I'll bite ya eyebrow off,' were seldom heard back in the mid-eighties. It's a real shame that when you think about an average teenager these days, this is the stereotypical person you envisage.

The purpose of this book is to make a personal account of what it was like to grow up on a council estate with no mobile phones, no Sky TV, no home computers and not a lot of money but bags of imagination. We didn't place emphasis on material items, although some of the lads did possess cool Nike windbreakers, compared to my Sheer jacket, and sweet Nike Air Max trainers. The Blue Door mentioned in the title of the project relates to the 3m by 2.5m roller shutter door where our group of friends used to congregate for a friendly game of football. The door was a rear entrance/exit to a now redundant dairy, located off a busy main road.

Several names will pop up throughout the book and we will be trying to find the very essence of these people, to see what made them tick and find out his or her lasting memories of Newcastle upon Tyne back in the eighties.

I'd like the following to take a bow:

Mr Jason Allison aka Popeye/Jay/Coco

Mr John Ingram aka Egg Heed

Mr Scott Smith aka Bun

Mr David Henton aka Gep

Mr Michael Fox aka Square Heed/ Flat Heed/ Teen Wolf

Mr Wayne Aldred aka Pacman

Mr Paul Durkin aka Flappy/Spinx

Mr Darren Patterson aka Furry Lamb

…and last, but not least,
Mr Neil Davis aka Beedie

We have tried to obtain information from all the above sources, to add more depth and knowledge to the piece. We hope we have captured the spirit of Cowgate, our native suburb of Newcastle upon Tyne. We hope too that you will enjoy reading the work as much as we have enjoyed writing it.

Flappy D

Chapter 1

"Those were the best days of my life"
– BRYAN ADAMS, Summer of '69

Meet Popeye and John Ingram

PAUL: I returned to live in the suburb of Cowgate when I was eight years old. I had lived there previously from birth until my second birthday, bunking up with my grandparents as my mother couldn't afford a place of her own. Times changed, my mother got a half-decent job and we were on our way. The six years in between took us to Stanhope Street, an area located near St James's Park, home of Newcastle United Football Club, and then to a fairly respectable estate called Blakelaw. Although my mother was very independent, she spent a lot of time with my elderly grandparents, therefore in the end it made sense making the move to be physically closer to them.

A lot of the family raised their eyebrows at the move, as Blakelaw was considered a far superior and safer estate than Cowgate, but in all honesty, my mother was never happy there. She had spent most of her life growing up in Cowgate, so the move was, thankfully, a happy one for her. She was back in her spiritual home at last. We moved to our new residence in Whitethorn Crescent during October 1980, although the house left a lot to be desired. The family we had exchanged with were new-age hippies and I can remember most of the doors, frames and skirting boards being painted black. Nevertheless, we did settle in very easily (after redecoration!). I was just starting my first year at a local primary school and I did not have any friends following the switch from my previous school and being an alien in a new area.

Even from a young age, I can remember Cowgate having a poor reputation. The estate was situated in the west end of Newcastle, about 3 miles from the City centre. Over the years, it had built up a dismal name for itself, having a selection of families with tough reputations living there. Unemployment was high and quite a few houses stood derelict. Crimes, including burglaries, were rife in the area. To coin a phrase, it was 'Thatcher's Britain' and local folk couldn't see it getting much better in the foreseeable future. On the flip side, this added to the character of the place

During my first couple of years in Cowgate, I hung around mainly with the friends I made at school. There weren't many kids of my age with my sort of interests knocking about in the area. I had spotted on several occasions, though, a skinny kid with dark brown spiky hair, talking to older lads at the end of the street. He seemed to have a keen interest in cars and always had oil-stained clothes, from being under a bonnet or under some motor vehicle. I plucked up the courage to talk to him one day and found out his name was Jason Allison. I also discovered that he went to the same school as me, but I was a year older so didn't really socialise with children in the other years. He told me he went by the name of "Jay" or "Popeye". This was a nickname he had acquired from his older brother, Raymond, because of an eye operation he had a few years earlier. He also mentioned that he was the youngest of five children, Ray being his only brother and Lynda, Sonya and Susan his other siblings.

I became good friends with Pops after this meeting and we spent a lot of time hanging out. With us being friends, I got to know his brother Ray a little better. He was a big lad in height and build, who enjoyed a good laugh and had a passion for cars. He was also the guy who christened me "Flappy".

I was born with an unfortunate birth defect - more embarrassing than anything else - but one of my ears really stuck out. I could probably have lived with both of them sticking out like the FA Cup, but only one was hard to bear. Because of this affliction, I always had long hair, to hide the protruding ear. Getting fed up with my hair one day, I decided to take my first trip to a proper barber, "Terry's", who was known for no-nonsense haircuts. I paid my money and asked for a mushroom cut, (all the rage in the early eighties). It became apparent during the cut that I had made a terrible mistake. I thought my ear had looked big when I had hair, but nothing could prepare me for the gargantuan sight before me. I would not have looked out of place as a satellite dish on someone's roof! I made my way home, very paranoid, and had the misfortune to bump into Ray.

'Last time I saw ears like that, I was watching Star Trek!' he proclaimed.
I ran off, trying to hold back the tears, while chants of "Flappy, Flappy," were being called from behind me. The name has stuck ever since.

I did eventually have my ear pinned back in 1995, but I suppose I will always be Flappy D to the lads. I also picked up the nickname "Spinx" for some obscure reason. One of my old school colleagues, Mark Richardson, called me by that name when we were playing with our Black Hole action figures one day back in 1979. It stuck with me and my friends call me Spinx to this very day. People have joked in the past that he meant to say "Stinks" because of my bad breath, but it came out wrong. I suppose only Mark knows the truth...

As we spent more time together, I began to notice that Pops was a fearless lad who would do just about anything for a laugh. He had devised a fun and exciting game of "Hedge Lobbing," which consisted of finding a decent privet hedge on the outskirts of a garden and proceeding to dive through it head first. Being a novice at this game, I tended to take the lower bushes at first, maybe 2ft in height, and just try to straddle the hedge, whereas Pops would find an eight-footer and glide straight through it. The game did have its downside, though, such as cuts from rogue bushes, or torn and grass-stained clothes. As we became older, the hedges got bigger and more people would get involved. If we took to a particular hedge, we could easily spend 45 minutes to an hour diving through it. Admittedly, this did cause a lot of damage to the owner's privet but we did try to keep noise to a minimum and, after all, it was only a hedge! I called time on this game when diving through a six-footer in the Fenham area, (a west end suburb of Newcastle); I had not checked the other side of the hedge, which was a cardinal sin. I believed, through experience, that a grassy fall would await me on the other side of the shrubbery. To my horror, the house was set down a flight of six stairs and an 8ft drop onto paving stones. My cry of bravery, 'whey hey,' turned to one of terror, 'ahhh,' as my back smashed off the cold concrete. Somehow I had managed to flip 180 degrees in flight! I stood up in a daze, bruised and winded. As I reached the top of the stairs, the rest of the lads were in kinks of laughter. I gave them the finger and never lobbed a hedge again.

After a few months of hanging around with Jay, he introduced me to a schoolfriend of his, who lived within spitting distance of us. John Ingram was a small, stocky lad who lived on the posh side of Cowgate. Now, I know that John will protest this until he's blue in the face and try to say he lived in North Fenham, but we all know the truth! John was an only child, like myself, and lived in a very nice semi-detached house near to the Blue Door where we congregated. His parents, Tom and Anne, were very likeable and friendly people, who always gave John the best of everything. He was the first person I knew to own a ZX Spectrum games console. He was also dressed in the best clothes: Adidas tracksuits, Kappa jackets and Nike Air Max trainers were never beyond his means. John soon found out he could not escape the nickname club and was subsequently dubbed "Egg heed" due to the unusual oval shape of his head. There was a television series on at the time, called "Spitting Image", a comedy show starring latex puppets and John reminded me a lot of the Andrew Lloyd Webber puppet. His head was not dissimilar to a coconut!

It was now the summer of 1982 and we were hanging around together as a threesome. Other lads such as David Henton, Lee Chamberlain and Scott Smith would join us for a game of "gates" or a proper game of footy on the local field. Gates was a game of football played in the street, using opposite garden gates as our goals. On several occasions, irate neighbours would scold us for volleying our caseball [football] off their front door or, worse still, their window. One particular gate used was that of an elderly lady by the name of Mary Wharton. She was actually the mother of former Newcastle United full back, Kenny Wharton. She didn't mind our using the gate, but at times got annoyed with the ball hitting her property. She did ask us to move, which, to be fair, we did for five minutes or so, then we would return when the dust had settled.

Now then, Mrs W had a bulldog, Shane, whose reputation went before him. It was a snarling beast with an uncanny desire for feet, ("pasties" as they were referred to in Cowgate). This day, we had the misfortune to cheese Mary off for the last time. After Popeye had half-volleyed a wicked shot off the post and then straight off Mrs W's kitchen window, she decided to release the pastie-munching hound. My ball landed in her garden and I made a quick hop over the fence to retrieve it. Just then, the door opened and this black blur charged towards me. I was helpless and just dived for the step, managing to grab the drainpipe. Shane made a lunge for me and connected with my left pastie. As our canine friend was a bulldog, there was some serious lock-jaw action going on. A surge of pain ran up my left leg as the dog's incisors tore into my foot. My shriek of 'Ahhh, ya bastard!' could be heard in the neighbouring streets as Shane went to work on my foot, riving it back and forth. Mary heard my Ned Flanders-type squeal and came dashing through her door. She managed to prise our four-legged friend's mouth from my foot after about five minutes. I was shaking and sobbing like a girl from my near-fatal pastie loss. My mother came out and started flipping, threatening to get the dog put to sleep. Mary yelled back about causing damage to her property and using her gate as a goalpost. I got dragged away into the house, still whimpering, with my mother still fuming. In all the shouting and confusion, I noticed Popeye had slipped off quietly, to let the carnage ensue. To think it was his volley which had caused all of this! I was taken to the local doctor's, had a tetanus shot in my backside in case of lockjaw and was sent on my way. Gates became a thing of the past after that and Shane "Bitey-Feety" Wharton became the most feared dog on the estate.

Another incident, not dissimilar to the one above, where Pops created the havoc then f****d off (ahem, disappeared), happened in the cruel winter of 1983. A few of us had congregated outside my house, playing snowball fights in the garden and climbing the hedge to keep ourselves amused on such a chilly day. I left the group and nipped into the house for a matter of minutes, to change my now sodden socks. When I returned, the garden was empty and the lads were nowhere to be seen. Curious at their disappearing act, I ventured outside my gate to see if they might have walked around the corner and out of sight. I stood at the angle of my street and the main road, peering round with an inquisitive look on my face. I rolled myself a snowball and started to head back to my house, before I was startled by a car screeching to a halt and a brick stuff-house of a bloke charging towards me.

'Think you're clever, you slimy little git?' he yelled at me.

'Huh?' I replied.

Faster than I could say "Frosty the Snowman", this Neanderthal man had grabbed me by the scruff of the neck, bent me over and proceeded to place his meaty size-nine steel toe-capped boot firmly up my backside, with the vigour of a force nine hurricane. I let out an almighty scream as the guy threw me to the ground like a rag doll.

'That mirror will cost me £20 to get fixed, you little so-and-so!'

With that statement, he jumped back into his Austin Allegro and sped off.

My mother had heard my squeal and came racing out of the house, as the car headed out of sight. Mysteriously, just then all of the lads reappeared from behind a neighbouring privet, trying to hold in their sniggers. I was still whimpering like a baby, cuddling into the warmth of my mother. I explained what happened and she considered calling the police. I calmed down and the incident passed.

'What happened?' asked Popeye.

'This bloke got out of his car and kicked me full belt up the bum,' I said.

'What did you do to provoke that?' asked Scott Smith.

'Nothing,' I replied. 'He said something about a broken mirror.'

'Whoops!' came from Popeye's smirking lips.

'What do you mean, "Whoops"?'

He proceeded to tell me that while I was away, warming my pasties with another pair of terry-towelling socks, they had been throwing snow and ice balls across the main road, trying to hit the other side. In the midst of this, Pops had bowled an ice ball with such ferocity that it had just missed putting out the driver's side window on the X88 bus, but had connected with a certain Austin Allegro's wing mirror. After hearing the crack, the lads had darted in every direction. Naturally, the guy had turned back and found yours truly, standing on the corner by himself, snowball in hand. The rest was history.

'You snidey sods,' I shouted. 'My bottom is like the Japanese flag!'

'Soz,' said Pops, 'but the look on your face when the gadgie booted you was a sight to behold.'

I was huffed for about half an hour but slowly came round and had a laugh about it eventually, although I did have a ring-sting for a few days following the incident.

Meet Popeye and John Ingram

Between finishing primary school and starting secondary school, I had made a couple of new friends in the shape of Lee and Lloyd Chamberlain. The brothers lived opposite my house and shared a garden path with the aforementioned Mary Wharton. The boys and their mum, Jen, had moved into the street a few months prior to me and my mother. My first memory of meeting the boys was the two of them playing with their remote control car in the street. I was fascinated at the time as I watched this small racing car dart up and down the road, making sharp manoeuvres. I edged my way closer to the boys, hoping that they would make eye contact with me and invite me over. Lee, the older of the brothers, kept giving me the odd glance, then would look away as our eyes met. Now standing only a matter of feet away, I summoned up the courage to talk to them.

'That's pretty cool,' I said.

'Not bad,' replied Lee. 'Gets a bit boring after a while.'

'We got it as a present off me Nana,' chipped in Lloyd.

'Would you like a go?' asked Lee.

'Yeah, I would love to!' I said enthusiastically.

We played in the street for a half hour or so, before the boys got called in. I found out in that time that they went to Montagu Primary School, which was about a five-minute walk from our house. They were aged eight (Lee) and five (Lloyd). The brothers' mum and dad had separated about a year earlier and Jen had decided to move back to Newcastle after a short spell living in Germany. We became very close after a few months of playing together, which also rubbed off on our parents. Jen and my mother would often sit in each other's house and have a natter over a cup of coffee.

Star Wars was the big thing at the time, and Lee and Lloyd had nearly every action figure and vehicle. Lee "borrowed" me his Death Star one time, for the last day of term. I was the envy of all my school friends!

I also remember Lloyd having a very bad complex over the Incredible Hulk series, starring Bill Bixby. Everything would be going swimmingly until the line, "Don't make me angry. You wouldn't like me when I'm angry," was muttered by Dr David Banner. Lloyd would jump out of his chair and dart out of the sitting room. Lee and I used to look at each other and shake our heads. We even tried holding him down a couple of times, but he screamed so loudly that we let go in the end. Something had to be done for Lloyd to overcome his fear, so finally the family resorted to bribery. Lloyd's Nana offered to buy him the Rebel Snowbase from the Empire Strikes Back, as long as he could sit through an entire episode of the Incredible Hulk. He took this as a challenge and, true to his word, he sat one Sunday evening and watched the whole lot. Lee and I were a bit miffed at the whole situation, but as the dust settled, we knew that Lloyd was well worthy of that Star Wars toy.

The family got offered a new home in the autumn of 1983. Jen had always been on the look out for a house closer to her parents in Gosforth and this presented itself in the shape of a three-bedroomed terraced house on Chatton Wynd. I can remember going to look at the house with Lee, Lloyd, their mum and my mother, when it sat as an empty shell. Jen was still unsure whether to take it or not and I was praying that she would refuse. Lee and Lloyd were the best mates in my life at that time and I didn't want them to leave Cowgate. Jen decided to take the house and it broke my heart. I really sobbed the day they left for Gosforth, as I felt they were moving a million miles away. (In reality, it was a fifteen-minute bus ride.) We still kept in touch and I would sleep at the boys' new house and vice versa.

I recall a time when, after watching John Carpenter's Halloween 1 and 2, Lee and I were anxious to see the third instalment. I got my uncle to rent it out of the local video store for us, as it had a "15" certificate and I was only allowed "PG" at the time. Lee came down to my house, excited about the third episode of the horror series. We settled down in my mother's room with a couple of bags of salt'n'shake crisps and I placed the video into our top-loader Panasonic VCR. It became apparent after fifteen minutes or so that Michael Myers wasn't going to be raising his serial-killing head in this movie. Instead, we were subjected to an hour and a half of stupid mind control masks and cheesy special effects. To say we were disappointed is an understatement. I apologised to Lee about this gross misjudgement and he seemed very understanding. Anyone who has seen "H3 - Season of the Witch" will surely agree with me. It was utter crap! I did make it up to Lee a couple of years later by getting Rambo: First Blood, part 2, on a pirate copy for both of us to watch. It was a bit grainy, but we could still make out Sly's chiselled good looks.

Fast-forwarding a bit ...Lee and Lloyd both grew into men of stature. Lee joined the army after school and made the rank of lance corporal. He has served time for his country in Bosnia and Kosovo. He now runs his own contract cleaning company in Ipswich, Suffolk. Lloyd spent several years working at the DHSS, before moving on to ASDA Supermarkets, where he trained as a store assistant.

We have been friends for a good 25 years and the friendship is still going strong. Unfortunately, tragedy struck on Monday, 11th June 2007. After complaining of feeling unwell, Lloyd collapsed in his sitting room. He was rushed to Newcastle General Hospital, where he was diagnosed as having suffered a massive brain haemorrhage. He spent eight days on a life support machine and, sadly, lost his fight for life on Tuesday 19th June. Although I hadn't seen him much lately, Lloyd had never been far from my thoughts. He was a talented musician, playing both guitar and keyboard. I had arranged some guitar lessons with him a couple of years before but, alas, they never materialised. I will miss him very much. He was a kind, gentle, wonderful human being, who touched everyone who came into contact with him. I wish I could speak to him one last time to tell him this: I miss you, man. Hopefully, you'll get to read this in heaven. RIP, Lloyd.

Chapter 2

School daze

PAUL: The last couple of years at primary school seemed to fly by and before I knew it, I was preparing my newly purchased uniform for Kenton Comprehensive. I had opted to go to this school as it was fairly local and a lot of my primary school chums had Plumped for the same one. After only two weeks at the school, I realised how much I hated the place. I had "backed" every book with woodchip wallpaper, been intimidated by several other pupils and the last straw was someone coming behind me between lessons and sticking chewing gum to my hair and blazer. I sat with my mother and cried about not wanting to go back. There was only one option available to me if I left Kenton. The term " out of the frying pan and into the fire" could not have taken on a more significant meaning. Although the school was named Blakelaw, it should have been known as Cowgate Comp, because of its geographical location. It had a bad reputation and that's why I had chosen Kenton in the first place. You've probably heard the one about new pupils getting their heads flushed down the toilet during their first week at a new school, (rites of passage), but at Blakelaw they put you on a bus and threw you head first into the River Tyne! I bit the bullet, had a chat with the headmaster and decided to give it a shot. How bad could it be…?

I was introduced to class 1G on a sunny but cool Wednesday morning in late September 1984. Mrs Graham, the form teacher, sat me next to a small, blond-haired lad called Mark Howe. I spotted a couple of familiar faces from my primary school and immediately felt at ease. My first week went smoothly and I made several new friends. As much as I liked my new school and acquaintances, I also found out that secondary school can be harsh as some of the lads chose to make people feel like dirt all through the year. Two lads in particular had an uncanny knack of picking on your vulnerabilities and exploiting them. I had many run-ins with them during my time at school. On one occasion, one of the lads called for me on the way to school. My mother went to the door, looking a little dishevelled from just getting out of bed. Immediately, he picked up on this and, when we got to school, proceeded to tell the whole class that my mother was shooting up heroin and that he had caught her "swinging from the lampshade." From that day forth, my mother was referred to as "Lampshade Swinger". This is just one of many burdens I had during my school life. All petty stuff, really, but they annoyed the hell out of me nevertheless.

One month after my arrival, during form registration, Mrs Graham entered the classroom with an arm around the shoulder of a scrawny little kid with mousy blond hair.

'Everyone, this is Neil and he will be joining our class from today.'
I gave him a quirky look and he just stared back at me a little nervously.

'I require a couple of volunteers to show Neil around the school, so that he is familiar with his classrooms and timetable,' remarked Mrs Graham.

'Stuff that, 'I thought and immediately bent under my desk, pretending to tie a shoelace.

'Paul… Paul Durkin, can you sit up, please?' asked Mrs Graham. 'I would like you and …Malcolm Pattison to show Neil around.'

It appeared that I, being the new kid, would be best suited to showing Neil round the school. Mala was to be there just in case I got lost!

'Damn,' I thought, but got up and made my way to the classroom door, waiting for Mala and Neil to show up.

Malcolm was a funny, stocky sort of lad. He also resided in Cowgate with his family. He was nicknamed "Fergal" as he resembled a shark. (Fergal Sharkey was an Irish pop star with former punk band the Undertones – get it?) His aquatic looks had made him the butt of many jokes but, rather than retaliate, he would just give you a slap and tell you to shut it.

During our walk around the school, passing the maths and geography rooms, I found out that Neil had moved to within a five-minute walk of my house. He had come to our school from Chevyside, in the west end of the city, and was already acquainted with some of my new school friends as he had gone to primary with a few of them. After twenty minutes of walking around, I started to get bored. I looked at Mala, he looked back and we both nodded.

Upon my introduction to the school some four weeks earlier, I had been shown around in the same manner. I remembered popping my head into the canteen, to check out that day's menu. When I turned round, my host had done a runner, leaving me stranded, with only a blank expression and thoughts of Irish stew.

We headed towards the school gymnasium, making small talk on the way.

'This is the gym,' I said. 'Quite dirty and old, but it does the trick for a game of five-a-side.'

I spotted a ball at the far end.

'Fancy a quick game?'

'Yeah, replied Neil.

'Will you run down and get the ball, please?' I asked.

As soon as Neil turned his back to retrieve the ball, Mala and I were off like a bride's nightgown. We bolted out of the gym and back to the classroom.

'Where is Neil?' asked Mrs Graham upon our return.

'I don't know, Miss,' I replied. 'He was with us one minute and gone the next.'

'Go and look for him now!' cried Mrs Graham.

'Howar, Mrs G, play the game. It's not our fault if he mysteriously got lost while on the grand tour of the establishment,' I exclaimed.

'Go now!' shouted the teacher.

'Alreet, calm down, you old coffin dodger,' Mala said under his breath, while walking sheepishly from the classroom.

Mr Pattison and I took a leisurely stroll around the school, before finally making for the gym. It was empty.

'Oh man,' said Mala, 'Mrs G is going to kill me!'

We headed back to the classroom, fairly worried about losing our new classmate, only to find Mr Davis (Neil) perched at his desk.

'Luckily for you two, he found his own way back. Now take a seat,' said Mrs Graham, glaring at us.

I passed Neil on the way to my desk and looked down at him. He gave me a quick smirk and quietly mouthed an obscenity before gazing away. He never dobbed us in that day and told the teacher he got himself lost. That was our first meeting and we are the best of mates to this day.

Halloween

I naturally introduced Neil to Pops and John, who were very curious about this new lad whom I had been talking about. The three of them didn't really hit it off at first, but the more time we spent together, the more they became accustomed to each other and soon the foursome was inseparable. I would call for Neil on the way to school in the morning and we would talk of arrangements for the evening. As the end of October drew close, a plan was hatched to make some money from the wealthier people in the surrounding estates. Halloween is an evening when children dress up, get their faces painted and hollow out turnips, (swedes to you Southerners), to make lanterns; that night the Jolly Sailor Monster Jig came into full effect.

'What are we going to do this year?' asked Pops

'God knows,' replied John, 'but it will have to be better than last year. We never made a penny.'

'The "penny for Halloween" song is rubbish,' I commented. 'We need something to make people smile and put their hands in their flippin' pockets.'

'How about coming up with a jig to mesmerise the homeowner into thinking he's watching Shakin' Stevens live at the City Hall?' suggested Neil.

'Sounds like a great idea,' replied Pops. 'Let's get to work on a routine.'

For one week solid, leading up to All Hallows Eve, we worked like mad to come up with a dance schedule to equal that of Michael Jackson's in "Thriller". To add to the effect, I wore my finest pair of Farah stay-pressed, a red Liverpool FC home shirt (even though it was bloody freezing), my smartest pair of white Nike cotton sports socks and my black slip-on "horse" shoes, (named thus because the loafer type sandal bore the emblem of a fine four-legged steed galloping across fair meadows). All I needed was a Soul Glow perm and you would have been pushed to tell me and MJ apart! The hard work paid off and the Jolly Sailor monster Jig was born on a cold October evening outside the Blue Door. We all looked at one another, gave high fives and smiled.

'Duridge Drive, here we come!' shouted John.

Duridge Drive was directly opposite my house, maybe 50 metres away, but it could not have been further away in terms of prosperity and wealth. The Drive consisted of four-bedroomed private houses, top of the range cars and, most importantly, money. Other than the main drag, which took about ten minutes to walk, eighteen cul-de-sacs ran off the core street.

The night arrived and we got into character. We managed to pick up some cheap plastic masks, 25p each, from Danny Kohli's Mini-Mart, located at the top of Cowgate. They were the last four in the shop. Popeye's was the Bride of Frankenstein; John's was a vampire; Neil had the wolf man, which resembled a German shepherd dog in heat, and I had a witch. Neil also purchased a hairy hand, which had more significance at a later date.

'How come I got the worst?' I wanted to know.

'Stop whinging, man. Does it really matter? No-one knows who's under there and there are nee mirrors around the drive, ya can see yourself. Anyhow, you should have been quicker to the shelf,' replied Pops.

We left the shop and made our way towards the Drive. We had one last practice run at the Jig, then we were off. We stood at the mouth of the street, peering down into the darkness, only the lamp-posts giving off the occasional shimmer of light.

We walked nervously down the first path and Neil stepped up to ring the doorbell. We waited…no answer. He rang again. Still no answer. In the end we gave up and moved on. The second and third houses brought the same result.

'We'll be lucky to buy two flippin' flumps at this rate,' said John.

We continued on to the next house, knocked on the door and waited. A light flickered on in the passage and we heard footsteps approaching the door.

'Here we go, boys, look lively,' said Neil.

A middle-aged guy opened the door, to be greeted by four 11-year olds standing in single file, pointing to the sky. The man looked skywards to see what we were pointing at, but then the penny suddenly dropped. Before he could say, 'No, thanks,' we burst into song.

'We're the witches of Halloween, ooh ooh.

'The ugliest you've ever seen, ooh ooh.

'We fly about at night and give you such a fright!

'We're the witches of Halloween, ooh ooh.'

The jig that accompanied the song was a complex set of dance moves, which included moon-walking, hopping backwards on one leg and flailing our arms around in a spooky manner. It culminated in all of our palms coming together, then our outstretched arms pointing towards our unsuspecting spectator. We completed the dance with a little 'Hey' just to add the finishing touch.

The guy stood inside his porch, motionless, assessing the high-energised monster mash he had just witnessed. Without saying a word, he placed his hand in his pocket and handed over 50p. We were over the moon. Fifty pence!

'We're going to dine like kings tonight, boys!' I screamed after leaving the guy's garden.

'Keep this up and we're looking at over 40 bar [pounds] between us,' cried Ingram.

The night was a complete success. We canvassed over a hundred houses that cold Halloween evening and made a grand total of £37.20. The jig was a triumph and we made a lot of people smile with our monstrous boogie. We did have the occasional rejection, such as people watching the routine, laughing and then shutting the door.

'Stingy so-and-so,' Pops would say after their door was closed.

'Aye, I'm out of flippin' breath and they didn't even cough up any coinage,' John would add.

'Stuff them,' said Neil. 'We'll come back at Christmas and pelt snowballs off their windows.'

'Keep a mental note of the house number, Pops, and we'll see if their Warm Seal double glazing can take the power of an ice ball in a couple of months' time,' I remarked.

One rather stuck-up lady, to whom we took an instant dislike, opened the door , gave us an icy stare and asked, 'Why are you coming around this area? Are you from Cowgate? Go away and stop bothering decent folk!' she shouted and then slammed the door. This really riled us.

'What did we do to deserve that?' asked Neil.

'God knows,' replied Pops, 'but anyone who needs a squirt, try to hold it in.'

We all looked at each other with a wry smile. We knew where Pops was coming from and we all felt retribution was necessary.

After we were puffed out and very content with the money we had made, we started back towards home.

'Ah, remember this house?' Pops reminded us. 'Follow me, but be quiet.'

We opened the gate with caution and headed towards the vegetable patch. We formed a half circle in front of the patch. In synchronised motion, much like our dance routine, we stood to attention, unzipped our pants and let the yellow river flow all over the old hag's cabbages. We shook ourselves off, zipped ourselves up and made our way out of the garden. We were twice as satisfied.

We sat under a street lamp and evenly distributed the money we had made.

'£9.30 each, boys!' said John.

'I never had this much money before in my life,' I commented.

'Who's up for a chippy?' asked Pops.

'Too flippin' right,' Neil replied.

We headed for Gorman's chippy, the finest fish bar in the west end of Newcastle, only a stone's throw from Duridge Drive. I bought a fish supper that evening and ate every bit.

'I don't often have chips, let alone fish and chips,' I remarked, while sitting outside, munching my cod.

'You won't have to wait long for the next one though, Flappy,' replied Pops. 'It's November 5th next week and you're going to be the Guy!'

Bonfire night

The week seemed to come and go very fast and, before I knew it, Bonfire Night was upon us. I drew the short straw and became the Guy. The principles were much the same as Halloweening. You would normally construct a Guy out of old clothes and newspaper, sling him across your shoulder and knock on doors, asking, "Penny for the Guy?" This year the chaps had decided to make the dummy more life-like and asked me to do the honours. I eventually agreed to act the part as I found out I'd spend most of the evening sitting on my arse. I put on my worst pair of Hi-Tec trainers, a pair of Geordie jeans, which were too small for me, and my Sheer windbreaker jacket, complete with a Mitre caseball in the hood for my head. Pops had drawn a face on the football, finishing it off with a gigantic ear.

'I have asked me dad and he said it was okay to lend the wheelbarrow,' said John. 'Sit your backside in there, Flappy.'

'Champion,' I replied.

We reached Duridge Drive with a sense of déjà vu engulfing us.

'Let's hope we have as much success as last Wednesday,' remarked Pops.

'Anything is a bonus,' I replied. 'I don't have a flippin' penny to my name.'

I climbed into the wheelbarrow and we were on our way.

We had a great laugh, going around the streets, although we didn't make as much money as the previous week. Sometimes Pops would take control of the wheelbarrow and fling me off kerbs, spinning the thing at the same time

'Pack it in, you freaking idiot,' I would shout. 'You're going to get me killed!'

We made about £20.00 in total that evening. Not a bad return, as we had a lot of no-shows (people who were out).

I was still sitting in the wheelbarrow when we neared the end of the Drive and I could hear whispering from the other three.

'What's going on? Can I get out of this thing? My backside is numb,' I exclaimed.

'One more house, mate,' answered John.

'Remember this one from last week? I'm sure the bloke gave us a quid,' remarked Neil, hesitantly.

I sat in the barrow, oblivious to what my three chums were planning. Before I knew it, Pops had used his weight to pin me down. I felt one of the others, I'm unsure who, grabbed the sleeves of my jacket and tie them together.

'What the hell is going on?' I screamed. 'Get off me, you bunch of Harries.' [Harry: rhyming slang for Harry Ramp – Tramp.]

Next thing I knew, the barrow was going skywards and starting to pick up some speed. The lads had lifted the wheelbarrow, with me in it, up into the air. I felt a quick jerk as I was flung from it; I ended upside down in a hedge, with my pasties pointing to the dark night sky.

'Howw – get me out of here, you bloody rarphies [tramps].'
I felt the blood rushing to my head, as I was propped up in a vertical position, sticking out of this privet. I could hear roars of laughter and footsteps disappearing into the distance.

'Help…Help…For god's sake, help…' I cried.
Silence fell around my ears and I became more uncomfortable. My head and neck were crunched up, with the football being in my jacket hood, and I couldn't release my hands, as they were tied together. I doubt even Harry Houdini could have escaped from this predicament. I tried to wriggle free, but to no avail. I must have been stuck in the privet for ten minutes before I managed to squirm free and fall from the hedge. After picking myself up, I spent another ten minutes manoeuvring my way out of the garden.

'Which way now?' I thought to myself.
I wandered around the bloody cul-de-sac for nearly five minutes, bumping into cars and tripping over several kerbs. Ultimately, I banged into a Ford Escort, setting off the alarm. The owner of the car ran from his house, to see this headless kid with no arms, pressed up against his bonnet.

'What are you doing, you little upstart?' shouted the man.

'Don't hit me, mister, I can't see a thing,' I replied.
He didn't take a blind bit of notice at my cries for help. He prised the football from my hood, my head popped out like tortoise's and that's when I felt the hairy side of a hand.

'Trying to hoist my motor, eh, you little git?' he said, slapping me across the chops.

'No,' I shouted, 'please listen to me!'

I proceeded to tell the man that I had been dumped in a hedge and had been roaming around like this for nearly thirty minutes.

'Let me help you,' the guy said at last.

'I'm going to kill them!' I wailed, as the man untied my sleeves and handed me the football.

'Who are you on about, son? The people who did this to you? Do you know them?'

'Aye,' I replied, 'they're my best friends.'

'What a shower of shits,' the man muttered, before turning and walking off.

I knew the chaps would head for one place only with wonga [money] in their pockets – Cowgate Service Station. This was the local petrol garage and we were friendly with the cashiers, Paul and Darren. The lads would often go in to spend what little money we had on sweets and crisps. I ran as fast as I could the short journey from Duridge Drive to the garage. I entered the forecourt and stopped dead when I reached the door. I pressed my face against the glass and saw Pops, John and Neil stuffing their faces with a wide variety of goodies, including Cornettos and dry roasted peanuts. I pushed the door to let myself in – it jolted and I froze. The thing was locked. I looked up to see the lads and Paul, the cashier, creased up with laughter.

'Let me in!' I shouted. 'Open this flippin' door now!'

'Calm down,' replied Paul. 'Where have you been? It looks as if you have been dragged through a hedge!'

A roar of laughter went up as I lashed out at the metal kick plate. 'Are you going to let me in or not?' I bellowed.

'Not tonight, son. Try another time,' said Paul.

I gave them all the evil eye and trudged off towards home.

I got 100 feet away from the garage when I heard a voice call,

'Flappy, come back. We're sorry.'

I turned to see Pops beckoning me. When I reached the door, Popeye was already inside. He looked at me and turned the key, locking the door again.

'Mug!' they all called out.

I was furious; what a bunch…

'I hope your next crap is a hedgehog,' I screamed, before kicking the caseball as hard as I could at the serving counter window. I turned around and ambled off towards my house.

The next day, I got an apology from the boys but saw no cash for my valiant efforts as the Guy. As Popeye put it: 'We were caught in a moment and could only see Bazooka Joe bubble gums and Wall's Feasts.'

Werewolf of Cowgate

I had made several new friends when I joined Blakelaw. Another lad whom I got to know was Michael Fox. Mick lived close to Cowgate playing fields, only a five-minute walk from my house. He was a cheery lad who resembled Ralph Macchio from the "Karate Kid" movie, only uglier. Mick had an unfortunate mishap when he was ten. He was knocked over by a car on a busy main road. His injuries were not life-threatening, but he actually landed on his chin. This made his head take on a cube-like shape, therefore we had no choice but to call him "Square head". Mick was a keen footballer and even wore his shin-pads to bed. Neil knew Mick before joining the secondary school, as they had attended the same primary. We started to knock on him on our way to school and had a good rapport with each other almost straight away.

One morning, as usual, Neil and I walked down his drive and rang the doorbell. No-one answered, so we rang again. We could hear a commotion coming from the rear of the house; it sounded like chickens in distress. We listened intently at the squawking and clucking coming from the back garden. Just then the inner door was flung open and a grey-haired man appeared in the porch.

'Is Michael in, please?' Neil asked.

He and I looked bewildered at the sight before us. The man was wearing a vest, which seemed to be covered in feathers. Also, what looked like a trickle of blood was running from his mouth to his chin. He started to speak, but only a growl came out.

'Tell Mick to catch us up,' I remarked, with fear in my voice.

Neil and I backed up the drive and started into a steady jog. We headed into the subway which was on our way to school.

'Did you see that?' asked Neil, panting, as we came to a stop.

'Aye, mate. I think Micky's dad is a flippin' werewolf,' I wheezed.

'I thought they only came out at full moon,' said Neil.

'Obviously, not the ones who abide in Cowgate!'

Neil and I came to the conclusion that Michael Fox Senior was a lycanthrope, a creature of the night, a werewolf indeed. There was no other explanation for the seven-inch sideburns, the feathers matted to his vest and hair, the stream of blood running from the corner of his mouth and the howl that came from his throat.

'Do you think Mick knows?' I asked.

'Of course he must,' replied Neil. 'I'm sure I'd be aware if my flippin' dad was scranning a couple of live chickens for his breakfast.'

'We must tread carefully,' I remarked. 'If we let this one out of the bag, come next full moon, we're dead.'

We agreed that we would talk to Mick on the quiet.

'That explains what me peg [mother] was on about,' I said. 'She mentioned that the price of chickens had shot up at Safeway, due to the poultry population declining around Newcastle. I'm flippin' sick of having Pek chopped pork on me Sunday dinner lately, because she couldn't afford a cooked chicken.'

'Mick's father has a lot to answer for, I think,' said Neil.

'I have a couple of crucifixes in the house. We'll have to melt them down to make a silver bullet,' I replied.

'Only one problem, mate. We don't have a gun to shoot the hairy bastard with!'

I gulped and we headed speedily to school, to contemplate our next move.

We decided to confront Mick in PE later in the day. I had just finished off with a game of indoor football, when I spotted Mick on a bench with a couple of other lads, waiting for their turn on the pitch. I beckoned Neil over and we cautiously approached Michael Fox Junior.

'Can we have a word, please, Micky?' Neil asked.

We sat either side of him, looking a bit apprehensive.

'Sorry to bring this up, Mick, but is your dad a flippin' werewolf?' blurted Neil.

'Eh, what are you on about?' replied Mick, with a startled expression.

I couldn't believe Neil had just come out with it and it took me a little by surprise. I started laughing uncontrollably and it took a good couple of minutes to regain my composure. By this time, Micky's team had been summoned onto the pitch and he had started a game of football.

'We'll catch him after school,' Neil said to me.

'I can't believe you just came out with it, man,' I replied.

'Nee good beating about the flippin' bush when our lives are at stake, mate,' he said.

We headed back to the changing rooms to shower when the lesson finished. I had started to get undressed when Neil tugged at my shorts.

'Look,' he said, pointing in the direction of the showers.

I turned and saw Mick going towards the communal shower area, wrapped in his towel. I struck me immediately that Micky had to be the hairiest twelve-year-old I had ever seen. He was covered from the base of his back to his shoulder blades in black, stringy hair.

'Do we want any more flippin' proof?' Neil exclaimed.

'Jesus,' I replied, 'and look at the size of his flippin' toenails! He could decapitate someone from 50 yards with those bad boys!'

Michael had the longest toenails I had ever seen in my short life. They must have been inches in length. Neil commented that we could even go surfing on those buggers. We contemplated the fact that Mick may have misplaced the nail clippers but decided this was inconclusive. With the evidence falling out in front of us, we had no doubt that our chum, our school colleague, was in fact a Teen Wolf.

It was the topic of conversation as Neil and I made our way home once the school day finished. We talked about how Mick's ears were pointier than the average teenager's and questioned why his incisor teeth resembled fangs. This had us speculating whether his mother, Joan, and his sister, Karen, were also participating in nocturnal poultry consumption.

We were nearing the subway when we spotted a distinguished cube-shaped head descending into the underpass.

'Look, there's Mick,' said Neil. 'Let's catch up with him and find out the true identity of the Foxes.'

We started into a mild jog and soon caught up with Mick.

'How's it going, mate?' I asked.

'Oh, you two again,' answered Micky, unimpressed.

'We're sorry for the questions earlier, but we were a little concerned after we talked to your dad this morning,' I said.

We went on to tell him about his dad's appearance earlier in the day and how we really thought there was no explanation other than his dad's being a werewolf. Mick told us we had it all wrong. Earlier in the morning his dad had been moving an old bed mattress and duvet into the back yard as they had bought a new, king-size divan. That was how he had feathers stuck to his vest.

'And what about the blood running down from his mouth?' I ventured.

'It wasn't blood, you idiot, it was tomato ketchup. He had just finished scranning a bacon sarnie,' said Mick. 'He must have dribbled.'

Quick as a flash, Neil quizzed him: 'What about the sound of chickens from your back garden?'

'We don't have chickens, for f**k's sake. The neighbours three down from us keep hens. That's what you must have heard.'

'And the growl from the pit of his stomach?' I snapped back.

'He has a sore throat. He must have had a bit of phlegm stuck in his windpipe,' replied Mick, now with a tad of venom in his voice.

Neil and I looked at each other, still unconvinced by Micky's explanation.

'Don't buy a flippin' word of it,' said Neil. 'This is the biggest cover up since the JFK assassination.'

'Are you flippin' daft, the pair of you?' hissed Mick. 'Myself, my fatha, nor any member of my family is a werewolf.'

'We'll see,' I said. 'Come next full moon, your dad is going to have a silver bullet fired straight up his arse. We'll see if he survives that, the bastard!'

Mick's face was now like thunder. He turned and stormed off.

'The pair of you are scopey bastards. Keep away from my door!' he shouted.

'The truth will be known, Mick,' I shouted back. 'No chicken is safe with your fatha on the prowl.'

I stood motionless with Neil as Micky trudged through the remainder of the subway and out of sight.

'Where do we go from here?' I asked Neil.

'Straight to the Evening Chronicle,' he replied.

That night, we discussed at length what would be the best course of action, to make Wolf Boy and the rest of his canine family known to the local community. We both feared for our lives and didn't know how to get out of this predicament. The silver bullet comment was just off the cuff and we never intended to shoot Mickey's father up his anus. We decided going to the local newspaper would be the best bet. We told Pops and John of our plan.

'I've always been suspicious,' said Pops.

'Yeah, the last time I saw sideboards that size, I was watching the Antiques Roadshow,' commented John.

'Aye,' said Pops, 'it looks like someone has stuck a couple of guinea pigs to the side of his head.'

I slept at Neil's house that night, with thoughts of full moons and chickens predominant in my dreams. The following morning, still half asleep, I heard snarling sounds coming from behind Neil's bedroom door. I sat up to observe a hairy hand with four-inch fingernails wrap around the door. I felt my heart pounding when, all of a sudden, a furry face appeared and let out a roar. I cowered under the He-Man duvet and screamed in terror as I thought Michael Fox Senior had come to dine on my lower intestines! My squeal made Neil's mum, Iris, who was downstairs reading the paper, jump and rush upstairs.

'What the hell's going on?' shouted Iris.

'Don't panic, mam,' said Neil. 'I was just playing a joke.'

'Don't flippin' eat me!' I shrieked from under the blanket.

Neil, in his wisdom, had decided to don the werewolf mask and glove which he had bought for Halloween, and scare the shit out of me. After I had calmed down, we explained to Iris how we thought the Fox family were creatures of the night.

'You may want to sit down, boys. There's something I want to show you,' said Iris, disappearing out of the bedroom and going downstairs. Moments later, she returned with a copy of the Sun. She laid the newspaper on the bed. Neil and I turned to each other in horror after reading the headline:

BILL: I AM A WEREWOLF

I got dressed, then sat and read the morning's paper, regarding Bill Ramsey from Southend. From an early age, he had experienced strange occurrences, ranging from blinding rages to high fevers and menacing thoughts. Of late, the visions and nightmares had become more powerful. One evening, events came to a head and unfolded into a terrifying incident. Bill had felt unwell that evening and decided to go to Casualty, just to be on the safe side. As soon as he entered, the episode started. He felt noises from his stomach working themselves up past his chest and into his throat. A large growl then came from his throat. This startled the nurses working the back shift and they rushed to help. His hands were starting to curl in a paw-like manner and he lashed out at a nurse who was running to his aid. Bill was now down on all fours and actually sank his teeth into a nurse's arm. His face had become contorted, like that of an animal – a wolf, to be precise. The police were called and it took a few to restrain Bill. He was sectioned and taken to the local mental institution for help. He eventually looked for aid at his local church, where a priest carried out an exorcism. He felt cleansed after the ritual and found peace with his inner demon.

'That was a bit intense,' I commented to Neil.

'Yeah, man. Nee wonder the Foxes are covering up. Michael Senior is bound to end up in St Nick's if word of that crazy man gets out.' (St Nicholas' Hospital was the local mental facility.)

'Maybe we've watched too much TV, mate,' I said.

'Aye, films like The Howling, An American Werewolf in London, and Silver Bullet do nothing to put you at ease,' replied Neil.

'But doesn't this just about confirm our suspicions?' I said.

'Maybe it does, pal, but I think we should keep our friends close and our enemies closer,' replied Neil.

I agreed with Neil and we made a pact to put this werewolf business to the back of our minds and to apologise to Mick for the way we had gone on the previous day. We also agreed that calling the local rag was out of the question if we wanted Michael's friendship back and didn't want our heads bitten off! I got on my trainers and we headed up to Mick's house. We rang the doorbell and waited in anticipation. I felt a tad nervous and butterflies engulfed my stomach as we waited what seemed like an eternity for someone to answer the door. Eventually, Mrs Fox pushed open the porch door.

'Can I help you, boys?' she asked, with a scowl.

It was obvious that Micky had filled her in on our suspicion that her family was a bunch of bloodthirsty rooster ravagers.

'Could we speak to Michael, please?' I asked.

'MICHAEL!' yelled Mrs Fox, at the top of her voice.

This made Neil and me jump back, startled at Mrs F's wail. We heard footsteps trudge down the stairs and soon, Mick appeared in the porch.

'Oh, it's you two. I told you not to call on me,' he said.

'Listen, Mick,' said Neil. 'We're sorry about the things we said. We didn't mean to offend you or your family.'

'The two of you are both crackers. Did you really think my dad was scranning live chickens?'

'Erm, no,' I replied hesitantly.

'Look,' Neil chipped in, 'we were both wrong and know we upset you with our comments. Can we just be mates again?'

We then explained how we had got the wrong idea about his dad even though it looked a bit suss. We had jumped to the wrong conclusion and we were sorry for our outburst.

'Okay,' answered Mick. 'As long as you've both apologised, I can forgive you. Give me a knock on Monday, on the way to school.'

Mick closed the door and Neil and I retreated off the drive.

'Think he bought it?' I asked.

'I hope so,' replied Neil. 'If his fatha's not a werewolf, then I'm a monkey's flippin' uncle.

We had decided to make peace with the Foxes for one reason alone – the next full moon… To this day, I still laugh at every full moon I see, because I know Fox Senior might be on a poultry hunt that evening!

Chapter 3

Eight little monkeys

NEIL: No matter what we found ourselves up to, way back when, summertime was tree-climbing season. The venue was to be the Tavern Playing Fields. The Tavern, known as the Tav, (good, eh?), was situated more or less slap bang in the centre of Cowgate. The Tav, for us carefree souls, was a fine recreation facility. In our eyes, the Tav was like Vegas or, as Pops would say, 'Like Vegas but totally different!'

Forget Nevada; the Tav was our very own dreamland. Here you had everything you needed; space to run and scream, space to hide and seek. There was space to fly away if you wanted to. Anyone interested or blessed with wings could go up and over the long green grass and away beyond the vast line of trees below, which formed a great, long, bushy L-shape. Just enough space, I guess, to be young.

In the football season, the Tav boasted three good sized footy pitches, with full size goals – no nets, because if there had been any, we would have had them away. (More about that later.) So, for mere pups like us, getting hit by some joy-rider out here was highly unlikely, even if this was the Costa del Cowgate.

More about the trees… If I had to hazard a guess, I'd say there were, from left to right, approximately 100 of those bushy old birches between us and immortality. A hundred 30-footers, all in a perfect line, waiting to be crossed by any fool brave enough to risk his life and bones. Well, we eight brave souls were more than qualified for this ridiculous quest and forward we pressed.

The rules of this insane activity were quite straightforward and simple. If any part of your body came in contact with the grassy earth, you were out. No argument such as:

'Ahh ha whey, me pasties only grazed the grass tops,' (Pops), or

'Come off it, Davis pushed me,' (Bun),

would be accepted.

If you fell, you were toast, with a sore ass for butter! And considering the number of trees, falling at the first hurdle could easily mean a five-hour wait, while your buddies were thirty feet above, re-enacting a scene from Gorillas in the Mist. Five hours plus! Seriously, TJ Hooker and Mr T and the rest of the flipping A Team could kiss our rosy little asses, once we fine chaps found ourselves tree bound. Back then we had so much fun, I heard we made the Goonies jealous. The world would just have to sit and wait.

Obviously, after many unsuccessful attempts to become kings of the jungle and failing, like the swines we were, it was clear that something needed to change. Thankfully, by the next attempt we had adapted quite readily to the task in hand. I remember Davie H, who, like Micky F, was one of the bigger lads in our gang of merry men, suggesting, (while hanging about 20 feet high on a single branch), that perhaps we should shift the chances of our getting beyond twenty trees by bringing in a few new weapons of destruction, eg maybe a rope or the odd long stick.

'How about we just bring a frigging ladder?' enquired Johnny Ingram (known as Chuck Berry) in his usual no-nonsense manner.

'Aye, why not?' agreed Pops, with a triumphant smile.

'Ooh, bugger this for a lark. I've had enough of hanging around with a bunch of cabbages!' replied Ingram, as he headed home in a strop, leaving a tree full of laughter.

Meanwhile, Davie H set off across the field, towards a gap at the far end of the surrounding fence.

'Where are you going?' shouted Micky F.

'I'll be back in a minute,' replied Henton. 'Just going to get me father's ladder.'

Looking back, Popeye always seemed to lead the way in our tree time madness. It was very normal to hear him heckling insults towards our general direction from at least four or five trees further on. He had an uncanny ability to grip and swing at the same time, in one movement. I can remember shouting, 'Hey, how the hell can he do that?'

'Pass,' replied Durkin, 'though I'll be sure to ask the swine once we catch up with him!'

More hysterics as I fell out of my tree from laughing.

The main question, though, still remains and lingers: did we ever make it to the end and achieve our deserved immortality? Did we hell? Then again, I doubt we ever needed to. Like those trees, the Tav belonged to us. As far as we were concerned, it was ours, and only ours, and with the Blue Door within eyeshot, just across the street, we rarely drifted far. And God help any poor unsuspecting fool who happened to wander onto our patch. We would be after him in a flash, screaming and waving our sticks as we sped. I expect that, from a distance, we resembled an out-take from the film Zulu. Only different..?

Football

Football! Don't get me started. If you were lucky enough to hail from any town within the North East, (Sunderland excluded), football was like walking and talking. For us, football was the air we breathed. Football was everything. It's funny, really, for as a child, I was never much taken with the sport. My father, as you can imagine, was panic-stricken. I don't doubt for a second that the prospect of having me fostered out or adopted was rarely from his mind. (Ha, only fooling, pops!) I suppose it was the sight of him launching himself backwards up and over our neighbour's pristine 6-foot hedge, after a Michel Plattini wonder goal in the 1982 World Cup final, which really set deep and pushed me on my way. And in turn, without knowing it, he had created a lifetime of future early evening privet-related fun for eight lucky young chaps. How grateful we were, dad.

Stamfordham Field (Stamfi) lay just beyond the huge, grey, spiky fence which bordered the Tav. Here lay our theatre of dreams and this was where we played most of our football. Even though the Tav had much smoother surfaces, for some reason we nearly always ended up playing at Stamfi, whose surface was more like the Atlantic Ocean in a force nine.

We would stand around for an age on one another's shoulders while Bun, being the shortest, or Micky (Square Heed) Fox took turns, wrapping masking tape around the goal crossbar, to keep our newly-stolen nets firmly in place. Once the stage was set, it was World Cup singles time! Again, the concept was simple – you had to score a goal to advance into the next round. For some reason, I, Davis – legend – normally did quite well in this particular game between boys. More often than not, I would find myself and others standing behind the goal, waiting with baited breath to see who would be disgraced and go out inside the first round of doom.

I can recall quite clearly one particular match. It was blowing like a bugger and pelting down from the high and mighty, and Popeye was playing for his life, desperate for a place in the second round, with only three people left in. Facing the walk of shame couldn't have been further from his mind, when he picked up the ball just outside the 18-yard box.

As the other two players backed off towards the goal, Pops suddenly dropped his trademark right shoulder and went all out for glory. As the rest of us behind the goal covered our eyes, Popeye burst hell bent into the 6-yard box and, sensing the sign of an imminent challenge, threw himself high into the air and crashed into the bemused keeper, screaming,' Haa-whey! Ref! Penalty!' as he rolled around on the ground in what seemed like intense agony. Meanwhile, those of us behind the goal were rolling around, inches away from spoiling our muddy pants.

With a little wink of his eye, Pops had the ball firmly placed onto the penalty spot, well before anyone had a chance to contest his plea.

And while the unfortunate keeper picked himself up off the wet grass, Pops had his hand high into the air above his head, testing the wind. For Pops, a place in the second round was soundly booked.

I suppose it would be accurate to say that back then, as kids we had only one dream, that is to say, a combined sort of dream. Like any other kids, all we wanted to be, of course, was footballers. Yeah, you know that dream too, don't you? It's crazy really, because most of us actually could have made the grade – no joke! We just never mixed in the right circles, the kind that get you noticed playing football.

Taking this into account, with our desire to become superstars of the future, it was only natural that, before long, we would seek to ply our trade on playing surfaces far smoother than the death trap that we were used to on Stamfi field. Before long, good old Popeye and Davie Henton had found our brand new home ground. Deep within the confines of Newcastle Airport and a 40p bus ride away, we happened to land upon a University site, which boasted – wait for it – eight of the flattest, smoothest fields that we kids had ever witnessed.

To us, this was very deep and heavy. Eight pitches with goals! And green nets! (Hmm, nets!) I'd be lying if I said we were not both humbled and visibly shaken by this perfection. Micky F needed a hug. Bun needed a hanky, for a change. Perhaps we all did. Once we had gathered ourselves and slipped into our Diego Maradonna footy boots, it was time to get our act together. Considering we'd spent a small fortune getting there by bus, we decided to make a day of it. Secondly, once we had finished playing for the day, we were without a shadow of a doubt, nicking the nets! I know this might not lie well with some of you, but to us it was rude not to.

On a lighter note, I can recall a time when our cunning net nicking caper hit the ropes big style. It was a particularly hot day in the summer of '85. As usual, after a day's festivities of lawn soccer, we decided that the nets were bound for a sweet relocation… Cowgate style.

One day, as we were winding down and with Pops in between the sticks, plying his trade, after what seemed like a routine catch, he decided to hang like a bat from the crossbar. Unfortunately for him, the wood snapped in two as he hung in mid-air. It smashed him a treat on the head, knocking him out instantly.

This unexpected turn of events had pretty serious consequences for the rest of us too. While Durkin and I pleaded with Pops to stay away from the light, Bun and the other lads were hanging from other crossbars on eight separate pitches, completely unaware that, some 300 yards away, their dear buddy lay out flat on the ground, unconscious and trying out his best starfish impression. It was only when a gent known as Hitman Kelly began to scream that I started to be concerned.

'What's your frigging problem, eh, Kelly?' I shouted. 'He's okay.'
It was then, as I turned to Durkin with a knowing smile, that I was met with that same vision of panic I'd seen in Kelly.

'F-f-frigging leg it!' he screamed in my face.
Dropping in unison from each goal frame with nets in hand, Micky F and the others suddenly began to run with all they had , dropping the nets as they fled. For just some 200 feet behind, four skinheads and a German shepherd cross hurtled towards us in a Ford pick-up truck, like a rust-ridden rocket from hell. Across the pitches they screeched, towards us and our depleted starfish pal and, more importantly, the only exit.

'Wake up, wake up, you bleeding cabbage!' screamed Johnny Ingram as the groundsmen roared even closer.

'They're only ten seconds away,' I remember calling, as the rest of the lads bolted over the fence.

Sitting up like a shot, Pops suddenly switched his smirk from me to them and, without warning, he was on his toes and over that fence, past me and the others quicker than a werewolf let loose on a chicken farm. The sight of him heading top speed towards Kingston Park via a very commendable eight-foot privet will stay with me for ever.

That was the last time we fine gentlemen ever stole nets!

Azlam and the mini-mart stand-off

I can remember a time when a few of us were having grief from this local guy who used to run the corner mini-mart. He was legendary in our area for his shifty sales techniques and even shiftier produce. Right opposite the subway stood Azlam's mini-mart and less! For one thing, any white kid was a thief, in his eyes. It didn't matter if the kid had cash on the hip. No, to Mr A, who stood a mere 5'5" in both directions, you were a filthy dog with bad teeth. One time, I purchased a bag of Walker's crisps which were three years out of date. His response to my concern was simple: 'Yes, of course I know dis crisps are out of date, That is why they are 10p cheaper than de normal price.'

If you're thinking 'Hey, the gypsy swine,' you're right. However, credit should be given, especially when credit is due, and in our eyes, Mr A was a rock. Completely unflappable. You could smash a Pringle golf ball at 60 miles an hour through his main glass front double window and the guy wouldn't even blink. Well, when we tried it, he didn't.

Even though it was a good twenty years ago, I can still recall that night like it was yesterday, which, for me, is pretty damn good. The so-called feud had begun many months earlier; it was nothing really major, either. Then again, with us it didn't need to be. For a while, Mr A had been buying returnable fizzy pop bottles from our dear selves, all at cost. If the return value of the bottle was, say, 30p, we wanted 30p back. Simple, right? Wrong! Dear old Mr A decided, after a brief spell of happy cash giving, to lower his fee from 30p a bottle to a shocking 5p, take it or leave it, strict cash offer.

There were other issues, such as, 'You nicked them for free, so you are lucky to get anything.' This philosophy of his cut very little butter in our soup kitchen, even if we were only thirteen years old. After this, it was simple, it was war!

We stood there together that frosty night, shaking in the cold, early evening wind on Stamfi field, directly opposite Master Azlam's empire and less. Two of my mother's friends, let's say Frank and Rosie, who lived next door to Mr A, left for a night out, giving us a wave. They were off to the formidable Ord Arms public house (known as a smugglers' paradise).

'Hey, are you totally sure this crap idea is going to work?' Johnny Ingram asked. 'Listen, all I'm saying is I don't want to go wasting my golf balls.'

'For flip's sake, Chuck, of course it's going to work,' snapped Davie Henton, staring across the field towards Azlam's. 'Look, it's barely a 40 foot drive.'

Meanwhile, some 45 feet away, Mr A sat contentedly on his usual perch, a stool behind the prized and beloved shop counter. He was blissfully unaware that, just outside and beyond the street and busy, tooting traffic jams, six young chaps stood waiting. Waiting they were, for a decent gap between the oncoming cars and City bound buses. Just six crazy young buggers, looking to tee off.

'Okay, Davis, the tee is yours. The traffic lights are on red, my friend, so let's be having you as quick as you like,' said Pops, rubbing my shoulders in encouragement.

And with the wind to my east, I swung like a baboon on speed.

'Aah, camel crap,' I whined, as my ball smashed into the metal railings at the far end of the field.

'There, you see,' yelled Chuck. 'I frigging knew this would happen.'

'Well, here's the nine iron, if you're any better, my egg-headed friend,' I prompted, handing over the club.

'Watch and learn,' smiled Ingram, flicking his jet black hair, as he took a swing, sending his ball a feeble ten feet in the wrong direction and straight in to the path of poor Flappy's buttocks, sending him high into the winter night.

'Aaargh, me frigging arse! You coca cabaña egg-headed swine,' whimpered Durkin, on the deck, while we all looked towards Azlam's with shaking heads.

'Nice shot, Mr Ballesteros,' quipped Henton, with a smile, while Durkin found his feet, rubbing his ass.

'Blow me!' replied Chuck.

'Hey, this is pony [a poor showing]' shrieked Pops. 'Anyone got some masking tape? I have an idea.'

After a short delay and in the failing light, we were ready to proceed. And while Cowgate roundabout ducked for cover, the games continued. 'W-w-whoops,' screeched Davie H as his ball hurtled straight through the bedroom window of the house adjacent to Mr A's store, Frank and Rosie's house. 'God-damned wind sheer,' he sighed, handing me back the club.

'Right, this time I will be true. Azlam,' I called with all my might, 'time to say goodbye to your windows!'

With the power of belief deep within me and the daylight about to blink out, I proceeded to steady myself. Mr A looked on from his stool and out through Pops's masking tape target circle, which now graced the shop front window.

A gap in the traffic appeared. Confident with my desired path of projection, I breathed in deeply, then swung. Like a bullet, my ball raced with the combined weight of six deranged souls, straight on through Mr A's upstairs bathroom window, taking out a half full bottle of Radox Moonshade bath oil with it and, unbeknown to me, half the bathroom tiles too.

As you can imagine, the perfect bath time moment, as promised by Radox Ltd, was, sadly, not to be the case for Mr A's sweet old mother-in-law. Her bath time bliss and calm, scented moment had, should we say, been somewhat unpleasantly interrupted. Waving her fists at us through the now altered window, she hissed, 'You bloody bastard! My sons, they kill you!'

'Good to see she's been working on her English,' agreed Popeye and Ingram, as we prepared to flee into the shadows.

Then something happened, something we had definitely not

seen coming. With bedlam still raging on the upper floor, Mr A, accompanied by his two rather big sons, who'd been upstairs, watching Eastenders, stood calmly, strolled past the counter, out through the shop door and onto the street, to survey the damage. We, sensing that a two-man baseball bat assault was possibly imminent, prepared to do the sensible thing and scarper. However, it was Mr A's hysterical laughter which stopped us in our tracks.

'What the hell's he laughing at?' shouted Bun, as we looked back.

Mr Azlam and his sons stood together, staring at the shop window, with its near perfect sticky paper target still all in one piece. The three of them then proceeded to chuckle their asses off.

Pointing to the window and giggling uncontrollably, he yelled, 'Hey, boys, I think you missed just a bit!'

Gazing in total disbelief, we looked at one another helplessly, while across the street, the three wise men jigged back and forth outside their shop in some kind of spooky Hindu triumph. Kissing the glass and with a smile, Mr A suddenly turned to us again and shouted, 'Bring it on, suckers!'

I felt the golf club being ripped from my grasp with urgency and force as Popeye burst past me, screaming towards the one remaining golf ball, which sat peacefully, still and alone, on its tee.

'Don't you frigging miss,' screamed Johnny Ingram. 'That's my last one.'

It did not matter now, as Pops hurtled forward, swinging the club above his head, like a windmill caught in a typhoon. None of us needed to say a thing. We all knew where our fate was now headed, as Pops swung with a roar, connecting perfectly with the ball. Like an arrow, his drive was both true and low. At first, it seemed too low to clear the same fence that had cruelly denied me a little earlier. But then, the ball suddenly rose by the inch it needed, as it screamed across the street.

Pops was now lying, with grass in his teeth, flat out on the ground, where he'd fallen. We all looked on in anticipation as Mr A pushed his two sons away from the white rocket's path, before hitting the deck himself, just in the nick of time, as the ball raced through the open shop door. Crash, bang it went, straight into a display of White Lightning cider bottles and Monster munch crisps, sending glass and 10p confectioneries high into the air.

'Our shop!' screamed our Asian chums, while they lay dazed on the pavement.

'Yeeeesss!' hollered Popeye from his place in the dirt, as we all raced over and held him up high into the sky.

I'll never forget that crazy night, when Flappy, Bun, Micky F and the rest of us danced the night away.

'Good old Popeye,' I remember saying, as we headed home to our egg and chips.

Good old Popeye – as if he'd ever miss! (Though at the time he never admitted it? He did hint some six months later, that at the exact point of impact he had both eyes firmly shut.)

Perhaps you'd believe me too, if I told you that when I finally plucked up the courage to head back over there to Mr A's, some three weeks later, for some penny delights, he only had our golf balls behind his counter, for sale at 50p each. Ha, I kid you not. Like I said earlier, this guy really was a rock.

Take a bow, Mr A, for you earned a tinge of respect from at least six naughty kids from the neighbourhood. Most people would have dialled 999, but not good old Mr A. No, he simply accepted that on this night he had been out-manoeuvred by six hungrier golfing chaps. And did dear old grandma ever find it within her heart to forgive Radox for failing to honour its guarantee of aqua heaven? Well, I just couldn't say. And while you have me on the subject, I can confirm that within the next 12 to 24 hours of trading in the Azlam empire, the purchasing price of White Lightning and out-of date Monster Munch did indeed soar by a very impressive 33%.

Business is business. Enough said.

Chapter 4

Reflections of Cowgate

NEIL: Walking through these same Cowgate streets, just two days past (Summer 2006), it both hurts and appals me that in twenty years, hardly a stone or boarded-up house has been touched. It's as though this place of my dreams and nightmares has been forgotten. Forgotten by time. Forgotten by you?

Surely, too many of life's stories and life's characters dwell in this empty, barren place; is our little world to just die and fall off the map without a whimper? 'Where is all the life?' a voice inside my mind screams. 'What happened to the friends and neighbours who smiled, who lived?' The same houses, I see, still throw out their unkempt gardens like sweet, wiggling children's tongues. For me, though, the light and laughter have been stolen.

I remember when I was about eleven years old and my sweet mum worked the early evening shift behind the bar at the notorious Windmill public house. Notorious, that is, to anyone who had never actually been there. I'd had it up to my back teeth with the usual ignorant remarks from kids at my school, who claimed that the Mill was a right dump, or the west end's version of the OK Corral. Ha, don't get me wrong. You wouldn't take the lady of your dreams there for, say, brunch. But hey, the ladies of my dreams were never around to be invited.

No, for me the Mill had everything. I'd sit by the bar on my trusty stool, while my momma chatted and served the various locals their conversation and drinks. Even as a small fellow, I noticed how much my mother, Iris, was respected. She knew how to handle both the smiles and the Friday night trouble, and the folk who came there liked her for it. The feeling of safety was never an issue, as I sat there at the bar in Cowgate's toughest pub, drinking my Coca-Cola, served with a happy wink from my mum.

Most of the regulars were either related to our family or, if not, they might as well have been. There wasn't a soul who didn't know my name in that dusty old place, with its broken pool table and fuzzy jukebox.

'Want a Coke there, kidda?' my Auntie Moira or Uncle Colin would smile.

They were usually joined at their table by Yvonne and Terry (Moira's sister and her hubby). Half of them played darts for the pub's ladies' team, including my peg [mother] and they were quite a side. My mum and a few of the others actually played for the County ladies' side, which was a bit special – like Eric Bristow, but different.

Hee, I recall one time when I played my mum at a quick game of 501 Down, for a joke and, to my horror, I won. As you can imagine, my mother failed to see the funny side of being trashed by a child in front of her pals. And while I proceeded with my merry sailor victory jig, my dear mum proceeded to kick my cheeky little ass. It was around this time that I decided that ladies, handbags and darts should, perhaps for the next ten years, be avoided.

It's a funny feeling that comes rushing in as I look back to those happy days. For if I'd claimed in class that I felt honoured to come from where I did, and to know the people I knew -the big scary people like Johnny Tams, (who was more like a giant teddy bear), and all the others who looked out for one another - my classmates would have had a good old laugh at my expense. However, like I said, they had obviously not been there, so what did they know?

The following people should, please, take a bow: Aunt Moira and Colin; Terry and Yvonne Cave; Johnny and Dawn Tams; Mark and Dawn Trotter; Ant and Dawn Brown, and the rest of the '80s crowd. If I forgot you, I apologise, for I never received your cheques! Ha ha.

Today, Cowgate stands motionless in time, trapped, I sense, by some invisible force, which has little urge for things such as laughter and life. The empty, barren homes stand cold and alone. At a glance, they remind me of cheap cardboard Hollywood cut-outs, like the ones seen in those old, low budget cowboy flicks. Houses meant for families look as though they could be lost or taken by the wind at any given moment.

Sadly, these homes have lost their families. In the early nineties, the City Council came together with a cunning plan to save our flagging neighbourhood. The motive was pretty straightforward. The area did have some troublesome and undesirable residents – whole families of them, some with more offspring than the Waltons! – and those people, were re-housed in other parts of town. Their former council homes were modernised and, with other houses that were built from scratch, were put up for sale as private investments.

To be fair, this simple idea should have worked to some extent. Unfortunately, though, it didn't. Much to blame was the extremely low value of the property market; back then, a three-bedroomed semi (without pool) in Cowgate would set you back a mere thirteen grand. So all that happened was that former rogues and thieves who'd been shipped out, to be forgotten, now found themselves back in Cowgate and, better still, they were now on the property ladder. Hmm, good work there, chaps. Or, as Homer J Simpson would say… Dohhh.

To be honest, the thing that frightened me most, growing up in Cowgate, was the thought of ending up like the older lads we knew in the neighbourhood. Don't get me wrong. It wasn't because of who they were or what they had. No, it was because they were still there. I'm talking about a group of guys, all in their late twenties, most out of work, most out of ideas too. Even at the age of fourteen, the thought of ending up like these lads terrified me. In many ways, knowing them showed us all what could happen if we ever gave up and accepted that this was our lot. I guess we were different. I guess we were lucky. And, like I said before, it wasn't because we thought we were any better than those older guys; believe me, we weren't. The only thing that did make us different, however, was the fact that we still had time… time to try to change.

Bike ride to Morpeth

PAUL: The hazy summer of 1986 was upon us soon enough and our life consisted of playing football all day on the main playing field or going on excursions and road trips around and beyond the City. This was commonplace during my youth and, as long as I had 20p in my pocket, I would go anywhere from Wylam to Whitley Bay. The World Cup was being played in Mexico during the months of June and July and we were keeping a keen eye out as a local lad, Peter Beardsley of Newcastle United, was representing England in the tournament. England had made it through the qualifying group stages and was due to play Paraguay on Saturday, June 18th. We were all looking forward to this game, as we had heard that Peter would be in the starting line up. The day soon came around and, early that morning, I stood at my gate, talking to Pops.

'Any plans for today, mate?' I asked.

'Looks like it's going to be a beauty,' replied Pops, staring up at the sky. 'How about going on a bike ride?'

'Sounds good, my friend,' I said. 'Oh, just one thing – I don't know if that heap of junk will make it any distance.'

The heap of junk I was referring to was the old boneshaker propped up against the side of my house. A couple of weeks earlier, I had a fairly decent racing bike which had developed a small puncture. My Uncle Johnny, the Del-Boy Trotter of Cowgate, offered to fix it and I, being very naïve, let him take the bike away for repair. Three days later, Johnny had returned with the rust bucket which now stood before me.

'Where the hell is my racer? 'I screamed.

'Calm doon and listen,' he replied. 'Your racer was beyond repair and I got a very decent swap deal with this fine model of a bicycle.'

'Beyond repair? Beyond repair? It only had a flippin' puncture,' I yelled back.

'There were complications beyond my control, when I removed the inner tube. Anyway, stop moaning, you whiny little sod, and try out your new cycle,' Johnny said.

'I'm not getting on that thing. It's a lass's bike,' I shouted.

It was the most feminine bike I had ever seen, and my idiot of an uncle wanted me to take it for a ride. All I needed was a picnic basket, a scarlet cloak and the big, bad wolf snapping at my ass, and I would have looked like Little Red Riding Hood. I moaned to my mother, who in turn moaned to Johnny, but it was to no avail. My racer was gone and I was stuck with this piece of crap which resembled a bike.

I subsequently found out, over the next few months, that Johnny had sold the racer for thirty pounds, spent the money in a public house and fished my "new" bike out of the local junkyard. It was such crap that even the local thieves wouldn't pinch it for scrap. With hindsight, I should have known better, really…

'Have you had a bash of it, Flappy?' asked Pops.

'No, mate,' I replied. 'I'm too embarrassed.'

Pops walked over to the bike, pushed it through my garden gate and started to pedal the bike up and down the street, occasionally doing no-handers.

'Hey,' he shouted. 'She handles beautifully and is easy on the ass. I'll tell you what, you ride my BMX and I'll take this baby.'

'It's a deal,' I replied.

I wasn't going to pass up an opportunity like this. Pops had got a top-of-the-range Mongoose BMX for the previous Christmas and was the envy of several of the lads. I had only ridden the bike twice, but it was a class above.

It was approaching 10.30am and the sun was bursting from the cloudless sky. The temperature was reaching 65°F already. We made our way to Neil's house, to ask him if he wanted to come along on our bike ride.

'Where are you going?' asked Neil.

'Haven't decided yet, but not too far, as I want to be back for the England game tonight,' I replied.

'How about the Airport, then Ponteland?' suggested Pops.

'Sounds like a plan,' I answered.

'Give me ten minutes to hoy on me clothes and brush me dominoes,' said Neil.

'We'll go and knock on Johnny and Micky, to see if they fancy,' said Pops. 'Meet you back here in ten,'

Pops and I called on Mick and John, with no luck. There was no answer from either house.

'Looks like it's the Three Musketeers,' said Pops.

Neil popped his head around his privet hedge as we approached his house.

'Road trip?' he asked. 'Where are the others?'

'No-one home, mate, so it's just the three of us,' I replied.

We counted our money and we had 98p between us. This would get us a snack and a drink, with change to spare.

We set off on the 14-mile round trip to Ponteland. We made a couple of stops and approached the airport by 12.00pm, cycling five miles in total.

'We're going to be there and back by half past one at this rate,' commented Pops.

I wiped the small beads of sweat from my forehead and let out a blow.

'What do you suggest?' asked Neil.

'How about it, chaps?' replied Pops, after scanning the surrounding signposts. He pointed at the post which read "MORPETH 11 MILES".

'I'm up for it if you two are,' said Neil.

'You know I am,' I replied. 'Let's go.'

'That's the spirit, boys. How about we cycle to Morpeth, spend a little time in the city centre, then jump the bus back to Newcastle? We can be home for 4 o'clock mat the latest. I'm sure the driver will let us on the bus with our bikes,' said Pops.

'Do we have enough money to get back?' I asked.

'Aye, I think it's only 10p from Morpeth to the town. We'll still have enough money for a Mars bar,' replied Pops.

'Good enough for me,' Neil answered.

We looked at each other, then set off. The ride was going very smoothly for about four miles. We had the soft wind in our hair and the gentle warmth of the sun beating down on our scarlet faces, as we rode our bikes at a leisurely pace. We came to a decline in the road, which hit a tight bend at the bottom, then veered off to the right. I have never claimed to be a top cyclist. I even had stabilisers until I was seven, that's how bad I was. I was at the back of our mini convoy as we started down the steep hill. Neil and Pops raced down the bank and soon disappeared around the turn. I cycled a tad faster, to try and catch up with them, but the faster I went, the less confident I became. I was unaware that, at the bottom of the hill, the road went into a small incline and then levelled off. I sped around the bend, hit the ramp at 20 mph and lost control of the bike. I flashed past Pops and Neil in a blur, before I hit a ditch and was flung straight over a thornberry hedgerow. The two looked at each other with startled expressions, as I vanished over the bushes, only my horse shoes on show, until I disappeared out of sight.

'Flappy! Flappy!' shouted Neil. 'Are you okay?'

'Speak to us, Flapster,' called Pops.

I found myself lying on my back, looking up to the clear blue sky overhead. I managed to prise myself into a sitting position and scanned the area, wincing as I turned my neck. I could hear the boys calling out my name as, eventually, I stood up. I was in a lush green meadow, with the odd dandelion scattered about. Nearby, there was a foal, grazing on the ripe grass. Heartened by this sight, I started to walk towards the fine four-legged steed.

'I'm okay,' I called to the lads. 'Just give me a minute.'

I had spotted a gap in the hedge but found myself walking in the opposite direction, towards the young foal. As I approached, it looked up, gave me a confused glance and starting grazing again. I patted its mane and stroked it gently.

'There you go, boy,' I said, feeding some grass to my new-found thoroughbred chum. 'Is your mother not abo…?'
I had hardly got the words out of my mouth when I heard the sound of distant hooves galloping towards me. I turned round to see this big colt heading my way.

'Shiiittt!' I screamed, as I bolted for the hedgerow whence I had come.

I could feel the warm breath of the galloping steed on my neck as I charged towards the thorny bushes. I sprinted as fast as my legs could carry me, knowing that my ass could be toast if the long-faced stallion caught up with me.

I managed to dive through the hedgerow just as the horse approached.

'That was a close call' I said 'I was nearly horse food!'

'Never mind being horse food' Popeye said, 'Look at the state of my handle bars!'

I glanced over at the BMX, to see the handlebar turned 180 degrees from the right direction.

'I'm not letting you back on my bike. Ride your own piece of junk,' scowled Pops.
As Neil helped me to my feet, I felt a pain shoot across my wrist.

'I think I may have knackered my wrist,' I said to Neil.

'Don't worry, Flappy, we'll be in Morpeth soon, then on the bus home.'

I slipped on my loafers and mounted the boneshaker. Surprisingly, it was easy on the buttocks, as Pops had mentioned, and I rode along at a snail's pace, resting my injured wrist on the handlebar. Pops eventually came around and started talking to me after twenty minutes or so.

'How's the wrist?' he asked.

'It's a bit sore, mate, but I'm sure I'll live,' I replied. 'Sorry about the handlebar. It's a good job you had the strength to straighten it out.'

'Don't worry about it, mate. I'm sorry I flipped on you,' said Pops.

We continued the seven miles into Morpeth, with my wrist still putting like a bad golfer. We asked for directions to the bus station and soon pulled onto the main concourse. I scanned the bus timetable and spotted the 518, which would leave for Newcastle in ten minutes' time. We cycled up to the stand, where people were now boarding the double-decker bus. Pops had by now dismounted and was pushing his BMX to the bus. I felt my stomach drop as I glanced at the driver's face. Pops had just set his front wheel down on the step of the bus when the driver barked, 'Where do you think you're going with that?'

'We're going back to Newcastle,' said Pops.

'Not on my bus, you're not,' answered the driver.

'Come on, mate, you have to be joking,' piped up Neil. 'We've cycled all the way from Newcastle this afternoon and me mate's gooshed [hurt] his wrist. I don't think he can cycle home.'

'Not my problem,' replied the driver. 'Bikes not allowed on buses and that's the rule. Now get off my bus; people are waiting.'

The driver closed the doors and started to back up.

'Thanks for nowt, you swine!' Pops cried to the bus as it reversed out of the bay and disappeared into the distance.

He extended the middle finger on his right hand as a parting gesture to anyone on the 518 bus who happened to be looking.

'We're shafted now,' I said.

'It's just after 3 o'clock,' replied Pops, looking down at his Casio digital watch. 'If we set off prompt, we can be home in time for kick off.'

'I don't believe this,' remarked Neil. 'There was plenty of room on that bus. He could easily have let us on.'

'Nee good moaning,' replied Pops. 'We still have 98p, so let's get a Mars bar and a drink, then head off.'

'Sounds like a top idea, man,' I sighed. 'Me throat's as dry as a dead dingo's donger.'

We headed to a little corner shop, bought our provisions and started back on the long trek to Newcastle. The sun was still beating down as we wound our way through the narrow country lanes and back onto the main drag which led us home. I nursed my battered wrist inside my t-shirt nearly all the way home, occasionally taking it out when cramp set in. Around 7pm, three beetroot-faced teenagers pulled up at the corner of Whitethorn Crescent, tired and worn out.

'I'm well done in,' said Pops.

'Yeah, me also,' replied Neil.

'Had a great day, boys, apart from that flippin' horse and the bus driver,' I commented.

'We'll have to do it again sometime,' remarked Neil.

We all shook hands and went our separate ways.

'See you both tomorrow,' shouted Pops. 'Enjoy the match!'

I got in the house, sat on the sofa and puffed out my cheeks. I managed to get myself motivated after about fifteen minutes and dragged myself into the kitchen, to search for the first aid box. As luck would have it, there was an elastic bandage, which I wrapped around my wrist.

After a small chat with my mam, I slowly walked upstairs and slouched down on her bed. We had only one colour TV in the house, a portable in my mother's room, and I wanted to take full advantage of the game in Technicolor.

The match itself was superb. England won 3-0 and Peter Beardsley scored one of the goals. The other two were scored by Gary Lineker, the prolific Everton striker, (now a TV presenter). I noticed that he was wearing a lightweight cast as he had injured his left wrist before the tournament. I gave out a little chuckle as I looked at his wrist, then at mine, both bandaged up…

Many fun times were had at The Blue Door!

From boys to men! Twenty years on and still as mad as ever, the chaps in 2009.

The Blue Door!

A legend in the making
...one Jason Popeye Allison Jnr.

Happy times, with my mum and sis, Spain '86.

Melanie Aldred: the girl who broke our hearts and taught us that personal hygiene and toothpaste should be embraced not feared.

A sprightly Neil and Durkin in 1985!

New York City
...the boys unite in 2008 for a American road trip to remember.

The way we were
...the boys (Spinx, Pops, Patters, Tootsie, Justin, Scott Fenton, Davis, Micky Miller) at Rothbury 1988.

Rothbury revisited ...the chaps head back to their spiritual home; this time with their very own sons and future adventures, 2009.

Chapter 5

NEIL: In my mind, at that sweet untameable age of twelve, little in the big old world of ours really seemed to matter.

My big sister Michelle and I usually fought like cat and dog. She had a good fifteen months on her little bro and back then, she also stole a decent four or five inches on me. Even at such a tender age, my big sis would not tolerate my bull. Seriously, she would see me coming from a week away; if she suspected her weenie namesake was up to no good, she would simply destroy!

I remember painfully one occasion when I went shopping in her new bedroom for a gift for my junior school sweetheart. I eased into my grateful pocket a pair of shimmering earrings, only seconds before Michelle's karate-like assault, when her left foot planted itself with venom between my cherries.

'Hi-yaaa!' she bellowed as I wailed on the floor.

Another time, I found myself locked in the larder cupboard, in the dark, while my dear sis waited on the other side. She was waiting for the sound of dog biscuits being consumed by her short-assed brother, before she would even consider letting him out.

Michelle didn't play! At school, if asked, she would often deny any knowledge of having a brother, let alone speak to him. Though come the time, which did come often, when some swine was pounding her little grub, out of nowhere she would appear. She'd come screaming across the yard, fists flying into any would-be assailant who dared hurt her dear little kid brother. No, even though she would never admit it, I knew that crazy bitch loved me, and how I loved her too. And besides, in those days, kicking my ass was definitely her job!

At the weekends, Michelle and I would usually hop on the No 1 bus at Slateyford, for the one-mile trip to sunny Scotswood, to see our dad and his new wife. Sometimes I'd race the bus, with our Michelle inside, all the way to my dad's, and most of the times I'd beat it, too.

Once inside Dad's place, you would immediately feel the warmth; the warmth from their fluffy carpets and boiling kettle, or that familiar heat on your lap from one of their many cats, who often came over to say hello. They did have one big, grumpy old tom-cat, Jo-Jo, who preferred to just give you a casual slap with his paw, or a quick nibble on your toes.

Babysitting

There was a time when a couple of my mum's pals foolishly enquired whether Mr Durkin and I could possibly watch their two sweet offspring for the evening. To Durkin and me, these folk needed their heads testing for even considering leaving their children, their babies, with us. However, after much deliberation and soul searching, and because we needed the cash, we decided to accept.

To be honest, the thought of babysitting a couple of brats terrified the two of us. This was uncharted territory, even though we were almost fifteen. Firstly, how the hell were we mere mortals expected to control and entertain a couple of kids widely known in the area as the Omen Two? Even the prospect of sealing £5 for a night's work did little to improve our mood as we gathered ourselves together before ringing the front door bell at 7pm prompt.

'Oh well, no turning back now, Durk,' I smiled, shaking like a girl guide.

'If they're looking for a war, I'll give them one,' snapped Durkin, determinedly.

'Ah, boys, you must be Neil and Paul,' screeched Mrs Moore, the children's mother, ecstatically. 'Mike, the sitters are here,' she called to her husband.

She asked us in, saying, 'The little ones are upstairs; they'll be down in a second.'

'They can frigging stay up there,' whispered Durkin under his breath, as we strolled into the devils' lair.

On first impression, all seemed well. I had a quick nose round and was pleasantly surprised not to see a complete tip, but a rather well kept abode, with all its doors and fixtures facing the right way up.

'Okay, lads, in the kitchen you'll find cakes and biscuits. There are plenty of sandwiches in the fridge,' continued the lady of the house.

'And what will the kids be having?' asked Durk, about 90% serious.

'Oh, silly you!' giggled Mrs M, nervously.

Feeling the tension ease, we took a seat on the sofa. The din from upstairs began to grow louder.

'Hello, boys,' hollered Mike (a Scotsman), entering the room, comb in hand. 'Right, first things first. If you have any trouble with those little devils, you just give them a slap.'

'No bother, boss,' I smiled, feeling invincible.

My response stopped the mother dead in her tracks and the two parents looked at one another then roared with laughter.

'You hear that, Mary? Got balls o' fire, these two wee chaps.'

Beep, beep, went their cab, and they were gone.

Turning to face a sheet-white Durk, I said, 'Just wait till I see my mother!'

'Not even the Bible could save us now,' he whispered as our young charges came screaming down the stairs.

'Who's the oldest out you two?' grinned the sweet little blonde girl of eight, while her nine-year-old brother looked on.

'Oh, that'll be me,' chirped Paul, standing up to shake the girl's hand.

'Well, you can have this!' she smiled, kneeing him squarely in the pods. 'My name's Samantha. Don't wear it out.'

'Oh, me pods, you little swine,' Durkin yelped in pain, falling to the couch.

'Now, hey. You two can quit this crap right now,' I shouted, feeling the rage.

Without flinching, Sam giggled, 'He's oldest, so he's in charge.'
The next second, they both sped into the kitchen, while Durk counted his balls.

'Hey, Davis,' my buddy groaned, 'I thought the Exorcist was bad enough, mate, but this takes the biscuit.'

'I hear you, mate. What the hell have we got ourselves into?'
Meanwhile, in the kitchen, Sam and Tom continued their food fight.

'Okay, mate,' I said, standing up. 'Time to show this pair of gypsies just who rules around here!'
Marching into the kitchen with fists clenched, I was met by a sudden Boom!! As the room began to spin wildly, I managed to reach out just in time, breaking my fall by crashing into the fridge.

'What the hell was that?' I croaked, clutching the side of my head as our two little demons burst through the living room and back upstairs.

'The little nutter just took you out with this,' said Durk, holding up a broken French stick.

'The little bugger,' I shrugged, finding my feet. 'Which one did it?'

'The same little minx, who just put my pods at ten to three.'

'Okay, mate,' I said, taking the sofa. 'Plan B. This is war. Now it's whoop ass time!'

'Tell me about it,' Durk said, looking up at the clock, which read 19.17. 'We've been here barely twenty minutes and look at us.'

Upstairs, the noise intensified as the kids had decided to use their folk's bed as a trampoline.

'Okay, bud, in here for a minute,' I said, walking into the kitchen. Once behind the safety of closed doors, (which we put a chair against, as a precautionary measure), I continued, 'Listen, it's obvious that we've messed up royally by taking this job, but, hey, let's not forget who the adults are here.'

'Try telling those little Hitlers that,' replied my flustered pal. 'But hey, what's this note on the oven door?

BOYS, PLEASE LEAVE TURKEY ON LOW HEAT AND TURN OFF AT 11-ISH

We'll see about that.'

He hiked the temperature gauge up to gas mark 9. 'Davis, my friend, say bonjour to your supper! The bird will be ready to go in two hours. Now let's sort out those two little monsters.'

Some time later, satisfied that we had covered all angles and armed with a handful of tea-towels each, we proceeded to crawl up the stairs on our stomachs. Our cunning plan was simple and well thought out. Basically, we would hit the enemy with an ambush, leading them into a false sense of security with the offer of cash. Once their misplaced trust was secured, we would then bundle them into the nearest bedroom and with the help of our cub scouts training, use the tea-towels as rope. We would secure, lock down.

'Okay, Durk,' I whispered, as we lay side by side, four steps from the top. 'Remember what we said downstairs? Nice and easy.'

'Check,' replied my Number 2. 'Time to take out the trash!'
As we found our feet on the landing, we were met with silence.

'Where are those little terrors?' we mouthed.
Like an invisible steam train, they came flying from separate rooms and grabbed Durkin and me by the ankles and dragged us off, screaming, in different directions.

As my pal and I rolled around the upper floor, trading blows with our assailants, I managed to slip young Samantha into a headlock. Following my lead, Durk pulled off a unique bear-hug tactic on the bemused boy of nine. We rolled them through the open door and on to the bed, then quickly slammed the door shut.

After some stunning tea-towel bondage action between the door handle and the banister, with the hour twitching 19.54, we had at long last achieved lock down.

'Say goodnight, children,' teased Durkin through the keyhole, while I leaned against the banister, tending my fat lip and bloody nose. 'Say a sweet goodnight to your little cherry asses, for tonight you demonic two have met your match.'

'Piss off!' came tormented Tom's response.

'We hate you!' chimed in young Sammy.

'No, you love us, my little rosebuds,' I said, taking centre stage.

'Tonight you will remember the names Davis and Durkin, for, children, these be the names which have kicked your cute little asses.'

'Now let's see how that turkey is shaping up,' smiled Flappy, high-fiving me as we headed downstairs.

I suppose it's accurate to say that night stayed with us and we laughed about it long after we got home to our beds. Also, I don't doubt for a second that we did the wrong thing by eating the turkey and blaming the kids. I recall that we almost ran out of the house the moment Mary and Mike pulled up in their cab. Poor Durk was so eager to vacate the establishment that he tripped over the dustbin on his way out.

However, I am grateful that Durkin's bear-hug manoeuvre came off that night. Who knows what might have happened if those two vicious little mites had got their way? Perhaps Paul and I could just as easily have left in a box that night, rather than in a cab.

I suppose to the outside world and to the untrained eye, what went down that night may seem somewhat hard to comprehend. But to us, stuff like that was the norm. Sure, we had heard the stories and horror reports concerning the ferocity of those two kids, but we still went. Come on, let's not be forgetting that Durkin and I were proud members of the fine gang of dreamers who secured that momentous price freeze in the world of returnable fizzy pop bottles – a feat which, I am sure, Mr Azlam would not dare to contest.

Meet Henton and Smith

No, in our minds we were invincible. How wrong we were.

During the summer, as previously mentioned, we would usually spend our days climbing trees on the Tavern playing field (the local social club), venturing far afield, or playing football on Stamfordham Road pitches. This last activity actually brought us into contact with a few lads who lived in the posh end of Cowgate. David Henton, Scott Smith and Wayne Aldred were all friends of friends. (Davie was friends with Micky Fox, Scott knew Neil from a previous primary school, and Wayne had become friends with John.) From the outset, we all hit it off and it wasn't long before we were knocking about with each other. So what can I tell you about each lad?

Let's start with David. Davie, as we called him, was the tallest of our group. At the tender age of fourteen, he stood head and shoulders above the rest of us. He must have been reaching 5'8" or 5'9" even then. He had a good build and was very strong; some of the lads discovered this when climbing into the boxing ring with him. He had fairly light hair, bordering on ginger, (he will say strawberry blond!) and he slightly resembled a young Jason Donovan, but with spectacles. Teenagers can be cruel, and with Davie being the only one with glasses, he got the nickname "Gep". Geppy was a slang word for glasses but we just shortened it. He also got "Speccy Rudge", a name devised by Neil. Davie took it with good humour but we knew where to draw the line. John once called him a name involving his hair colour and glasses and ended up feeling the strength of Davie's sleeper hold. He was into American wrestling big time, (WWF – Hulk Hogan, Andre the Giant etc), and had picked up a few moves while watching the programmes on television. After this incident, ginger and speccy were never mentioned in the same sentence if Davie was about.

Davie lived only a few doors from Micky Fox, on Ponteland Road, with his mum, dad, and brother Peter. We spent many a night sitting on his couch, eating mulligatawny soup and watching Hulk Hogan slam dunk some unfortunate lightweight, such as Randy Savage, into the canvas. Thanks, Dave, I still love that soup! Davie was and still is a very decent lad, who likes a laugh and a joke.

Moving swiftly on brings us to Scott Smith. Revell Terrace was never the same after the Smith family moved in, during the summer of 1987. John, Sandra, Scott, Beverley and Karl made up the family. They had moved down to Cowgate from Westerhope, another suburb in the west end of the City. Neil had recognised Scott one evening, while playing out. They got chatting and the rest is history. Scott was a very likeable lad who, like John, always had the best of everything. He was a stockily built kid. At 5'2", including his spiky hair, he was definitely the smallest of our pack. He wore his mousy blond hair with a centre parting, therefore comparisons were made with the Hooded Claw from the Penelope Pitstop cartoons. This, however, did not become the name by which he is known even now.

One night, I was invited to sleep at the Smith residence, so packed my finest pair of PJs and my rabbit slippers. I got comfy for the night in Karl's bed, as he was sleeping out at his Nana's. During the night, I was woken by what I thought was the mating call of the Indonesian Speckled Great Tit. I rubbed my eyes, puzzled by the sound ringing in my ears. I got up wearily and approached Scott's bed. As I got nearer, the sound got louder. I leaned over and listened. Picture a person snoring quite loudly, followed by a pause and the word "Kaa". I realised that the noise was coming from Scott. The next day, after a restless night, I questioned him. He confessed to having had his adenoids removed when he was younger and that was why he snored like that.

'Sounds as if you've got a blocked up nose,' I said. 'You need some Lockets.'

From that day on, after the lads had been told, Scott was known as Bun (Blocked Up Nose). He didn't speak to me for a while and I was never invited to sleep at his house again. He was also given other nicknames occasionally – Strepsil or Vicks – because of his nasal impairment. He took the names in good spirit eventually. There again, he had no choice!

Tea for three

NEIL: Moving back to yet another time of happiness and laughter, I smile when I recall the days when I, Flappy and Popeye used to fine dine at Bun's stately abode. Yes, come rain or shine, every Friday afternoon the three of us would set a table in the tranquil ambience of 2 Revell Terrace.

To be honest, the fact that Bun never invited any of us over for an early evening meal every Friday did not seem to matter to us at the time. Actually, I forget how the tradition started. All I remember for sure is that around 2pm on a Friday afternoon, Bun's dear folks, John and Sandra, hit the supermarkets with a vengeance. These guys came back with everything: ice-cream, assorted fizzy drinks and mountains of food, glorious food.

On one particular afternoon, Flappy, Pops and I sat indoors with Bun, watching Back to the Future 2. The proceedings were innocent enough, as Michael J Fox flew around on his skateboard. Suddenly, John and Sandra came in, laden with groceries, and we three visitors switched our attention from the flickering television set to the new delight that had kindly entered our hungry little lives. As Bun watched on, Pops, Durkin and I slipped out of the living room and into the dining area, where we beheld a mountain of food.

'Could we three assist you in putting away these fine delicacies?' quipped Durkin, licking his lips.

'Oh, thanks boys, that would be very kind of you,' smiled Sandra, leaving the room.

'Now we can go to the pub,' John smirked, as the two happy shoppers headed through the door, to claim their prize of a refreshing liquid delight.

'Don't mention it,' grinned Popeye, as we ushered them down the hall

We spotted that Scott was setting up the VCR for some forthcoming attraction. We joined him in the sitting room, made ourselves comfortable and had a chinwag for about ten minutes. Popeye then grimaced, put his hand to his forehead and puffed out his cheeks.

'You okay, man?' I asked.

'Not feeling too well,' Pops replied. 'I've come across all queer and feel as if I'm going to puke.'

'Get upstairs to the bog if you're going to throw up,' yelled Bun. 'Me mother just paid twenty quid to get the carpet and three-piece cleaned. She'll dee her nut!'

Pops nodded at Scott, then gave me and Neil a quick wink before disappearing upstairs and locking the bathroom door.

'Hope he feels better soon. Nowt worse than seeing Popeye off colour. Wonder if it's something he ate,' said Neil. 'Bit draughty in here, Bun. Mind if I close the living room door before you stick the film on?'

'Feel free,' came the reply. 'I'll put on a couple of bars of the fire as well.'

As Bun bent down and tended to the fire, Pops slipped open the bathroom door and tiptoed down the stairs. In stealth mode, which an SAS soldier would have been proud of, he glided past the sitting room door and into the dining room. A "click" came from the door as Pops turned the key and locked himself in. Nothing now stood in his way between the pantry and the cooker. Just as he liked it! Bun fiddled about with the fire for a little longer before it ignited. He then sat back in his chair with a concerned look.

'No noise coming from up there,' he said.

'I think he may be having a breather. He didn't sound too good. He's probably sticking his nappa [head] out of the bathroom window for some fresh air,' answered Neil.

'Aye, you're spot, mate,' replied our bunged-up friend. 'I'm just going to pop round to the garage for a Cornetto. Won't be long.'

Neil and I looked at each other with surprise and delight. Past experiences in the Smith household had taught us that Pops would usually cook up the first thing that he came across in the freezer. With Bun out of the way for a few minutes, that was our window of opportunity to pick what we wanted off the menu. We gave a knock on the kitchen door and waited. Everything went silent for a moment, then we heard the "ping" of a microwave oven finishing its cycle.

'Pops, Pops, let us in. Bun has gone to the garage and we want to choose our supper,' cried Neil.

We heard the door being unlocked and Pops peered around the door, with a Kellogg's raspberry pop tart hanging out of his mouth.

'Hurry up and choose,' he said. 'The oven's been on for five minutes to warm up.'

Neil and I headed straight for the chest freezer and looked inside. After a quick rummage around, I came up with three waffles, a portion of McCain micro-chips and a pack of Bernard Matthews golden drumsticks. Neil, on the other hand, Plumped for the 6oz steak with battered onion rings on the side. Pops had found a nice piece of cod fillet, which he was cooking up with a bit of parsley sauce and broccoli.

'Right, get out, and if Bun asks, I've taken a walk around the block for some fresh air,' said Pops.

Neil and I scuttled out of the kitchen and back onto the sofa. A few moments later, Bun reappeared with a mint Cornetto in one hand and a can of Diet Coke in the other.

'Sorry, I didn't have enough wonga to get you owt, lads,' he said.

'Nee problem, Bun,' I replied.

'Pops has just left; he'll be back soon,' Neil added.

'I'll start the movie now,' said Bun. 'He'll just have to miss the beginning.'

We began watching a grainy, pirate version of Robocop which was direct from the Middle East, (Bun had connections). Neil and I were a bit on edge, as the smell of a meaty rump steak started to waft from under the dining room door and into the sitting room. I gave Neil a worried glance. Just at that moment, there came a knock on the front door. Bun jumped up and peered through the sitting room window.

'Doesn't seem to be anyone there,' he said. 'I'll just go and check, to make sure. If those little upstarts down the street are playing Knocky Nine-door, I'll boot them right up the backside.'

He "paused" the VCR and made his way down the passage, then opened the front door and looked out. Nothing. Scratching his head, he continued to stare into the darkness. Then, with the speed of a panther, Pops opened up the dining room door and did a flying karate kick into Bun's lower back, throwing him out of the house and into bushy privet.

'Quick, shut the flippin' door,' hollered Popeye. 'Our nasally-challenged friend is spread-eagled in the hedge!'
I ran quickly and slammed the front door shut. I listened to the groans as Bun pulled himself out of the bushes and back to his feet. Then he started banging on the door and cursing.

'Let me in, you bloody tramps,' he wailed.
I stood shaking my head at what I had just witnessed. Pops had bolted out of the kitchen and through the dining room, and had let loose a fierce flying drop kick which Jackie Chan would have been proud of.

'Now, gentlemen, if you would kindly be seated, supper is nearly served,' said Pops, in a posh, butler-like manner. 'The soup of the day is golden vegetable, and there is a fine selection of breads from the continent.'

Pops had executed the plan to perfection. Just as the vegetable soup was simmering, he had let himself out by the back door, climbed the wall and knocked on the front door, then bolted back round to the rear of the house, knowing that Bun would answer at the front.

With Bun banging on the door, Neil and I took our seats. Pops was now wearing a nice wrap-around novelty apron, with printed bra and suspender belt on the front. He placed the soup in front of us and smiled.

'Bon appetit,' he said, serving us our first course.

We all sat at table and got stuck in to the soup. We dipped in crusty rolls and French bread to make the soup more pleasurable. After finishing, Pops took away our bowls and remarked that he would be two shakes of a lamb's tail. Aromas wafted in from the kitchen and my mouth started watering. Within minutes, our main course was served.

'Thank you, Mrs Smith, for what we are about to receive,' I muttered to myself.

Popeye laid the food before us and we gave him the thumbs up in approval. I tucked into my golden drumsticks, adding a touch of salt and vinegar. This was a meal fit for royalty

Unbeknown to us, Bun had made his way round to the rear of the house and, as I was finishing off my last mouthful of micro-chips, his fist banged heavily on the dining room window

'Open the door now,' he screamed.

Pops walked casually to the window, bent down to Bun's level and gave him the extended middle finger.

'Sod off, Bun, you little bag of excrement,' said Pops, closing the curtains. 'Can't have him staring at me while I'm scranning.'

Neil and I just stared at each other then burst out laughing. We finished off with dessert, a nice piece of Black Forest gateau, which hit the spot.

With Bun still knocking on the window, screaming obscenities, Pops rose from his chair and said firmly, 'Gentlemen, our time here is done.'

We sat up, rubbed our now full stomachs and headed for the dining room door. Pops cleared the table and left a pile of dishes the size of Mount Everest next to the Smiths' sink. He then quietly opened the back door of the house, before tiptoeing out and joining Neil and me at the font door.

'The door's open, Scott,' I shouted down the passage.

We then made a dash for it, finding it hard to run through laughing and having full stomachs. The three of us stopped short of the subway, doubled over in hysterics. We never saw Bun for a couple of days, lying low after our feast, but we heard he spent 45 minutes washing up and was grounded for a week, for eating £20 worth of food at one sitting. Suffice to say, he was always cagey about letting us back into his house following this incident, but it did recur several times when he let his guard down and failed to lock the dining room door. Thank you, Scott, for making three hungry 14-year- olds very full.

Chapter 6

Buffet

NEIL: For whatever reason, growing up, we all liked our food. Don't get me wrong, I'm not talking about a family kind of sit-down. It was more like short bursts. I remember when Durkin's ma would be out at work and he'd set his watch and give me a 60-second window of freedom to eat as much as I could muster, before slamming the fridge door shut and kicking me out. One time, Pops proudly demolished two litres of vanilla ice cream well within that one minute of opportunity.

I mean, it was crazy. After a while we couldn't even go into somebody's home without at least getting the frying pan going, whether we knew them or not.

However, it's safe to say that this dining frenzy really came into its own on the occasion when Durkin, Pops and I first attended a wedding. And no, before you say it, it hadn't a thing to do with the bridesmaids. It was the sight of the buffet that set our hearts pounding. Eight feet long and brimming with pristine savoury pleasures!

I shall never forget Pops shoulder charging a rather large chief bridesmaid out of the way, when those immortal words, "Ladies and gents, the food is now served," came over the mike. Popeye managed eleven plates that day, compared with me and Durk, who tied on eight. No mean feat for a 12-year-old. After this, a wedding was, for us, an event not to be missed. I even started asking my mother and her friends if they knew of anyone who was thinking of tying the knot. Jesus, we even gatecrashed a few, with Micky F and Davie H doing a speech at the end of one particular ceremony, to thank everyone for coming.

We really were a right group of hungry sods. I suppose, though, that our true defining moment in buffet style wonderland came about when Durkin and I actually managed to leave a wedding function with the buffet table. Well, I should say almost managed… We were cruelly apprehended at the top of the stairs by the rather unimpressed bride.

After this case of buffet mismanagement, we decided to lower our standards to a far more reasonable level ie by trying to beat Popeye's four-year record of eleven cleared plates. Something that, I'm sad to report, never quite happened. Ha, even now, when we all get the chance to meet up at some wedding or christening, all pleasantries are forgotten the second they turn on the mike. Seriously, if it came to it, I would trample my own mother to secure pole position at that sweet buffet table.

As the years continued to fizz on, our combined desire to eat other people's food kept up a steady pace and by the age of fifteen, any one of us could knock up anything, even a soufflé or a lamb cutlet dinner for six. To our eyes it was simple: if it was free, we'd eat it.

Let us now meet Darren "Lamb of a Thousand Furs" Patterson. I recall with bitter glee how, in the sensitive spring of 1982, Master Patterson Junior denied me the chance of signing off the Cowgate junior schoolboy soccer league with a well-deserved hat trick. In those days, Furry and I were Cowgate FC's version of Beardsley and Cole and on us hung our whole school's high hopes of a mid-table-like finish. It was on this occasion that my dear young chum cruelly robbed me of my impending victory parade by nipping in front of me three times in quick succession, (after I had rounded the keeper), and poking the ball home. Cult status was denied me and I slipped out of focus, while Darren was hailed as a god. Twenty-five years may have passed but I still say those frigging goals should have been mine!

Aged only nine when we met, I liked Darren the second we bumped into each other. It was that familiar smirk of his which won me over, one that has never changed. Named "Furry" because of his short fluffy hair, which had a lamb-like softness, re-named "Lamb of a Thousand Furs" within an hour of meeting Lord Durkin in the fleeting summer of '85, Darren proceeded to evolve slowly within those young tender years. Like young Bun, he now stands a mere five feet tall, and his once jet-black hair has turned grey.

Perhaps the sweetest left foot in the business for three decades, Furry also stole the spotlight in the Newcastle quayside discotheque arena. Without doubt, he was the finest mover I have ever observed. Darren, not shy when it comes to showing off his talent, can often be seen dazzling the crowds at our dear Nobby Solano's quaint yet seductive night-spot, the Cooperage, deep and well-hidden (well, it was), within Newcastle's bustling quayside.

I suppose Furry has remained so close a friend for all these years for one solitary reason – his ability to just be himself.

Ladies and gentlemen, I give you Furry… a lamb… a friend… a gent!

Chapter 7

Meet the Smythes

NEIL: 'They're over here!' screeched Jennifer Marjorie Smyth on that fateful summer morning in 1987. 'They're over here in their tent, with the milk,' she shouted to the passing police car. It was the same police car which, just ten minutes earlier, had chased John and me for the last mile and a half through the sleepy morning streets of Cowgate. Meanwhile, back within the safe confines of our tent, John and I shared the heroic tale of our close encounter of the officer kind with a bemused Durkin and Pops, whose idea it had been for Chuck and me to venture into the cruel morning air to get breakfast.

'Ahey, we only just shook the copper off,' gasped Ingram.

With our prize of a pint of semi-skimmed and one of orange Sunbeam unloaded onto the deck, we suddenly stopped, silent and still, as the sound of soft footsteps came up the garden.

'Who the frigg's that?' whispered Pops and Durk, slipping under their sleeping bags.

'Yes, that's right, officer. They're in there with the milk,' croaked our buck-toothed aggressor.

'The gypsy old goat,' the four of us whispered in unison as our tent zip suddenly slid up with a whoosh.

'Ahhh, hellooo there,' chimed the swine in blue, shining his torch in my face. 'Oh, and here is the milk. You're both nicked, lads.'

He grinned, placing a hand on my and Chuck's shoulders, and winked as he led us out of the tent, while Durk and Pops remained invisible.

'That's right, officer. Take them away. Trouble, they've always been trouble!' continued Jennifer.

'Give it a rest, will you,' I whined, shaking my head as the old bag stared with glee from behind her fence. 'Nobody likes a grass, Jennifer. If I were you, I'd make peace with your windows,' I smiled, heading towards the parked Panda.

'Nasty old cow, that one,' remarked Officer Bowden as we took our short drive to Gosforth Police Station.

'You've no idea, Sergeant,' I went on. 'The whole flipping family are proper seeing each other as well.'

'Ahey, he's not kidding,' chirped Chuck. 'They're worse than those bleeding Waltons on the telly!'

'Aye, we heard that too, son,' shrugged Officer Bowden as we roared up Ponteland Road and beyond.

This so-called war or, if you prefer, feud had been brewing for a long time. Old Jennifer, the youngest of three sisters, had, I suppose, the major beef with our band of merry men. Yes, it was safe to say that Jennifer had hated us boys from the very second she had set her wonky eyes on us, some two years previously. The thing about Jennifer that really hacked us off the most was her distinct lack of ability to reason. I mean, this crazy bitch was totally out of her tree. Naturally, I say this in an unfacetious way. Though it seemed that this soup-for-brains syndrome had not simply satisfied itself with our dear old Jen. The Smyth clan were the laughing-stock of the neighbourhood, owing to their unsightly appearance and their constant meddling. Although at the time I was a little young to be aware of it, I can now see and understand why folks had a problem with a family of two brothers and three sisters, all of a certain age, living together.

Firstly, you had George, the younger of the brothers, in his mid-fifties. He walked fast but unsteadily because of a limp. He worked at the local Tavern Inn, where his duties included emptying ashtrays and checking out the asses on the chaps while he cleaned the amenities.

Standing a mere 5'2" tall, old G sported an unsightly hump on the top of his back, which indeed brought the whole Quasimodo look off to a T.

Next, you had Alan. Very little remains known about old Al. Slightly taller than young G, Alan was about sixty. He usually went about his business unheeded and, to be truthful, he never gave us kids any trouble. Bless him.

Now we move on to the sweet sisters. Joyce, like Alan, led a reasonably quiet existence. Although she shared the Smyth family's slouch, I expect she wasn't such a bad old girl. Well into her sixties, old Joyce had a rather pleasant smile and was, let us say, the little mouse of the family.

And now, with the children safely and soundly asleep, I can introduce the gruesome twosome.

Let's start with Olive. What can I say? Olive, who was built like a bull, was short and squat. Well into her fifties, this old girl was made for bother. Old Olive was fearless and loved a ruck; the kind of lady who could sense mayhem a month away. The old bat would prove a real asset to her backward family when the heat was in the air. In a word, a right nasty pastie!

Finally, there's long thin Jennifer whom you have already met. In her teens, Jen could have had endless work in Hollywood as a witch's stunt double, thanks to her harrowing resemblance to the broom-flying kind. Old J had caused us boys to spend many a night locked up indoors, grounded and not allowed to roam the streets, falsely imprisoned because of the lies and tales from her poisonous lips.

I forget how, never mind why, this spiteful old trout had decided to wage an unholy war against Cowgate's fantastic eight. You know we were good kids deep down. Old Jennifer and Olive would grin at us from the street below, while, because of their words, we were incarcerated behind our bedroom windows on those long, school-free summer days. After a time, it had become a right pain in the ass. It wasn't as if we could blame our parents for being taken in by those two conniving gits; our folks were just doing their job. It seemed for a while that we were beaten and would simply have to take it.

Added to this, a year earlier, old George had tried to force his way into our tent, in the dead of night, to shake us up. It all made my inner fire burn.

So, two nights later, with the stars above our cheery little heads, we sat curled up together inside Spinx's Uncle Johnny's empty dog kennel, which happened to be the size of a small skip. (Uncle J lived next door to our tormentors' semi-detached council abode.) With the wind possibly to our east, we young souls started to hatch a cunning plan. Boom! Boom! Boom! Oliiivvve!

'Hey, this stuff is crazy,' I began. 'It's gone on long enough.'

'Tell me about it,' sighed Ingram. 'My mother nearly killed me when she got me back home!'

'I hear you, lads,' shrugged Durkin. 'The worst thing is, I wouldn't mind if we'd done half the crap those gypsy cows have accused us of.'

Changing the subject, Popeye chirped, 'Hey, nee wonder Monty (Uncle Johnny's German shepherd) never comes in here.'

'Huh, what're you getting at, Pops?' queried Durk.

'All I'm saying is nee wonder Monty never comes in here. The poor bugger would never find its way back oot!'

'Well, let's see you build a better frigging dog hutch,' snapped Spinx. 'Stevie Wonder would struggle to do a worse job.'

'Will you two shut the hell up,' I intervened. 'Jesus! We are here because of those Hicksville fogeys next door, so can we please get on with it?'

'I was only saying…' groaned Pops, as Bun and Wayne Aldred almost followed through from laughing.

Two nights later a plan was hatched.

I shall never forget that night. My feet dangled aimlessly, some 20 feet up, through the leaves and branches. Behind me, the eminent Popeye Allison shared my branch and we smiled.

'Hey, this is gonna be mint, totally mint, chirped my pal, glancing across the empty street, towards the front door of the Wicked Few's house, and back to Durkin and Bun, occupying the next tree.

Meanwhile, deep within a house some 100 yards across the street, a family moved. Brothers and sisters shared the night. Borrowed blankets covered the windows and protected the gibbering residents from the gaze of the modern world outside.

Two trees over, John "Chuck Berry" Ingram shared his branch with the flattest head in Cowgate – the one and only Micky "Teen Wolf" Fox. Lastly, but never forgotten, in a fine birch, some 20 feet over and right opposite the side of the Smyths' house, Davie "Down in two" Henton took a leafy view with Master Wayne "I think I'm well in there" Aldred.

Twenty seconds later, while the night grew darker still, Popeye crowed out his bird of prey signal 'Ooooooooo' and at once it had begun.

First to go was tree number 2, Durkin and Bun. Steadying themselves, the boys of the forest slowly began to take up the slack on their fishing line, which spanned from their very own sweet little palms, across the sleepy street, and was knotted firmly onto our unsuspecting inbred chums' door knocker. While our brave duo gently heaved, the rest of us held our breath, too afraid to blink.

The perfect door knock was achieved. As Durk and Bun quickly allowed their line to go slack again, the distant clunk of footsteps could be heard unmistakeably, heading down the bare wooden hallway towards the front door. The hall light was flicked on and the front door swung open. A startled Alan Smyth peered out.

'Er, hellooo, can I help you?' our old foe chimed.
Scratching his head in bewilderment, Alan stared long and hard across the street, towards the parked cars and sniggering trees. With a humph and a shrug of the shoulders, he shut the door again.

'Who was there?' croaked Jennifer in the distance.

'Oh, no-one, just the wind,' came the reply.
Across the street, four trees shook with laughter.

'It frigging worked!' shrieked Durkin from his tree.

'Sssh, lads,' whispered Chuck. 'Okay, Popeye and Davis, your turn.'

Taking our dear, gallant chums' lead, Pops and I carefully heaved our slack line tight. Knock, knock! This time, the head of the pack, the formidable Olive Marie Smyth, burst through the door and scowled at the night.

'Who is it?' she screeched with venom. 'Hello, is anybody there?' She was now joined by a curious Jennifer, who set her eyes wobbling into the night. Then, once again, Bang ! slammed the door.

Instantly, as arranged, Durk and Bun reapplied the weight to their line, bringing a perfect successive double knock before Jennifer even tuned out the light.

Straight away, the door heaved open, almost coming off the hinges, as an enraged witch screamed, 'Alaaan!'

The first part of our plan was proving to be a pure poetic success, so for the next ten or fifteen minutes we sat happily in our trees, while the enraged hillbilly five continued to search the perimeter of their garden with torches. Twenty more minutes passed before the baffled siblings were safely back behind the mysterious knocking door and we were ready to proceed to stage two.

Like a perfectly tuned orchestra, we began our swan-song.

With great care and precision, Henton and Aldred moved their line, which was neatly secured to the open upstairs bathroom window at the side of the house. Slowly but surely, the window began to clunk and clang into a steady drum beat. Feeling their moment, Ingram and Fox, who had been the most patient, made their move. Taking the weight, rat-a-tat went the open bedroom window at the front of the house, now in harmony with Henton and Aldred's. We others followed their lead in an instant, as Durk and Bun, and Popeye and I pulled onto our lines with everything we had, causing the front door to knock insanely.

The residents began to scurry and panic. With the four-prong attack now firmly giving it large, the front door suddenly burst open and

George rolled out across the grass like a beach-ball, onto his back. Next flew Jennifer and Olive, who both raced barefooted out through the garden gate and down the dark street, screaming wildly at the top of their voices, 'Helppp, somebody help! We've got f-f-frigging ghosts in our house!'

As the ensuing mayhem continued to unravel, we slipped silently from our nests and left the exceptionally mild summer night to enjoy the show, crying with laughter as we went, like never before.

Boxing

I recall one time when my sister and I were down at my dad's, playing in the sunshine with some of the local kids in the long, narrow street. I got pally with this kid who owned a couple of pairs of boxing gloves and at once the vision of Popeye and Micky F going the distance on Stamfi field, like Creed versus Balboa, flashed through my mind as a bolt from above.

After some tricky negotiations, I managed to persuade the bemused owner that his gloves (his brother's in fact) would be both well looked after and much appreciated up there in the neighbourhood of brotherly love – Cowgate. I promised him also that I'd have them back on his doorstep bright and early the very next morning. Hmm. Whoops!

What happened next was quite strange; the lads and I sort of went on a three-week boxing crusade. With the stage set, we had seven young fellows dreaming of immortality, seven fighters from the 'hood seeking to knock the living hell out of each other. The greatest prize in sport, it seemed, was just a black eye away. And like Highlander, but different. There could be only one.

Stamfi field... Bout one... Early on it had been decided by a majority vote that Stamfi field, our mutual brotherly home, should be graced by the opening championship bout. We even had a Championship belt. Well, I nicked a Power-Ranger toy belt from my neighbour's 5-year-old kid.

The prize ring, consisting of an empty milk crate in each corner, was almost ready. Pops and the rest of the chaps took care of the finishing touches. This basically meant propping a broken broom handle inside each milk crate and completing the whole project with a borrowed washing line. Thus we had a perfect square and, hey presto, our boxing career was born.

The rules, like most of our scams, were well thought out and simple. We decided on the punch for a point basis and a three-round bout. With everybody happy, we wrote our names on tiny pieces of paper and proceeded with the draw. At the time, there were only five of us in attendance: Pops, Bun, Micky F, Davie Henton and I. Davie, the biggest and baddest of our lot, was bookies' undoubted No 1 favourite to land the title, so if my dream of reaching the final was to be realised, I'd have to avoid my specky pal in the draw.

While Pops, who had decided he'd be the referee, rolled up his sleeves for the impending action, Bun made the draw.

'Ladies and gents, can I have your attention, please?' called our nasal chum as he picked the first piece of paper from Popeye's baseball cap.

'The first to fight will be… Davis… V… er, me!' he chirped, sliding into his gloves.

'Phew, thank the Maker,' I thought to myself as I readied myself for battle.

No disrespect to Bun, but I was delighted to have missed Micky F and Henton, who were both twice my size. The final, it seemed, was reachable.

Three bruising rounds later, Bun and I stood dazed and battered in our respective corners, waiting for the referee's crucial verdict.

'Folks,' cried Pops excitedly, 'we have a winner. In the blue corner, Scott "Nasal" Smith… 54 points. And in the green corner… with 56 points, our winner, Neil "Mushroom helmet" Davis!'

I'd made it. The final was my prize and I just needed Micky F to dispose of Davie H in their bout, to have any hope of my landing the greatest trophy in sport and being the king of the top field!

'Well done, pal,' smiled Bun, taking his place next to me outside the ropes as Henton and Micky slipped into the ring.

'Who do you think's gonna steal it?' I murmured, as Pops stood between the two heavyweights, quoting the rules.

'Micky F in the second,' grinned Bun, as Popeye sounded the bell. As the crowd went wild, Henton and Micky skipped around the ring like butterflies on speed. Then, boom! as Micky's head flew back with a fizz.

'Take him, Fox,' screamed Bun, as Micky bounced off the ropes. Two blows later, Micky flew out of the ring via the rope and milk crates and Henton punched the air in delight

'It's all over,' screeched Pops, as Micky lay sparked-out on the grass.

'Ladies and gents,' he screamed to an imaginary grandstand crowd,

'the final has been decided... Neil "Nee skin" Davis V Davie "Rudge" Henton.

'Micky, you hopeless tart,' I moaned, slipping on the gloves, while he picked himself up from the grass.

Henton, with a knowing smirk, lifted the rope with his foot, allowing me to enter the ring.

'Okay, Henton, prepare to kiss your ass goodbye!' I chirped foolishly, trying to unsettle the champ, while Pops again re-enacted a scene form Rocky IV.

'All right, lads,' continued Popeye. 'No rabbit punches. No holding, and when I say "Break", I mean "Break".'

'Don't worry, Pops,' laughed Henton. 'There'll only be one punch thrown here today!'

I responded with 'You vill lose!' (Ivan Drago –R4), as the bell rang.

Again, my devious plan was perfectly simple. For the first two rounds, I would go toe to toe with the big fella, trading blows and taking his finer punches. Then, with the third round about to play out, I would lull Mr H into the corner of the ring, feigning injury. Only then would I open up on him with a frenzy of lefts and rights, with the force and speed of a very young Sugar Ray Leonard. Sadly for Mr Henton, that would be lights-out time.

Two and a half minutes later, I was greeted by fuzzy friends and felt an almighty humming sensation in my jaw.

'W-w-what the hell just happened?' I croaked, lying flat out on my back.

'You got knocked oot,' laughed Bun and Popeye.

'Huh? When? What round?' I enquired, finding my feet.

'What round? More likely, what bloody second?' smirked Henton, picking me up off the dirt.

'Put it this way, Davis, you lasted about as long as it took his fist to reach your chin,' smiled Bun, and they all began laughing out loud.

'Nee way, Spanish waiter. Lucky punch, more like,' I groaned. 'Oh well. Well done, champ! I guess I'll let you take this one.'
If I'd ever wondered what it felt like to be smashed in the jaw with a sledge hammer, I knew now!

Three days later, we were ready for bout No2.

Alarmed at hearing he'd missed out on the first bout, Durkin (who had been on a sleep-over in delightful Gosforth) insisted on becoming the main attraction at the second meeting of leather and fists. Unfortunately, I had lost in a rematch with Bun the previous day and Henton, who still held the belt, refused to fight again until he felt a substantial challenge was on the table. Micky F was still on his sofa in a semi-coma from his first bout and Johnny Ingram was in sunny Benidorm, drinking cheap margaritas and no doubt chasing the waiters. This left only Popeye interested in bursting chops.

Bout two... Sonia (Popeye's sister) Allison's front garden...

'Okay, you two. As you're aware, we are looking for a good clean fight here,' I smiled. 'Let's keep it clean and simple.'

Meanwhile, as Durk and Pops went hell for leather on the tidy lawn, a small crowd had congregated around the perimeter of the garden. The bout slipped into the third and final round and only two points separated the lads.

'Go on, son, knock his bleeding head off,' wheezed some old git of seventy plus.

'Come on, Jason,' squealed Popeye's brother and sisters.

My announcement crackled over the imaginary mike, and the home crowd booed loudly when I awarded the fight to Durkin by three points.

'The referee's a bastard!' a group of charvas bellowed out from across the street.

'Hey, this is getting ridiculous,' I stammered to my two bruised pals.

'Aye, come on,' agreed Spinx. 'Let's wait in me mother's till these gypsies do a hike.'

About an hour and three cups of Typhoo later, and with the coast clear, we proceeded back to Sonia's garden for another bout. With another three rounds behind me, I was looking at my third successive defeat, but Durkin sealed his second win in quick succession by jabbing his way to a cute four points victory. It seemed that Mr Henton might have found his ideal opponent.

'Hey, Durk, if you beat Bun tomorrow, Henton's got to give you your shot at the belt,' said Pops. 'Listen, lads, I've an idea how we can land Durk the belt without even stepping through the ropes with Mr H.'

Overnight, a treacherous plan was hatched by three chums, in a back bedroom within a stately abode at the business end of Whitethorn Crescent. And first thing next morning, a hasty battle of wills and might was devised, to take place between our new great white hope, Durkin and Mr Bun "Smoking Joe" Smith – a battle which would later be referred to as the Rumble at Revell.

Ding ding went the bell at 11 o'clock prompt and, without a punch being thrown, Durkin found himself breezing out in front with a twelve point lead. In the third and final round, with less than twenty seconds remaining, he was hanging on with only a one point advantage. He was trapped in the corner, gasping for breath, as Bun moved in for the kill. Taking my lead, with a quick glance to his left, Pops, the referee, screeched TIME! sealing Spinx's place in history. With this, he too was now Davie Henton's challenger for the right to be King of the Ring. With three wins under his belt, Durkin was, officially, the Beast of Cowgate.

'Hey, something here smells dodgy to me,' shouted Bun, as Popeye and I did a victory dance around his back yard, to mark Durkin's rise to the top.

'Dodgy? Dodgy how?' puffed Pops, finishing off his jolly sailor jig.

'Ahey, too frigging right,' continued Bun. 'I was on top for three rounds and just as I'm about to finish him off, you scream Time.'

'And what are you doing the jig for, Popeye, when you're the ref?' enquired our nasal chum, throwing off his gloves and bringing our celebrations to a premature halt.

'This is nonsense, Bun, and you know it,' I intervened. 'Surely you're not suggesting that Pops and I were swayed in our decision.'

'All I know,' continued Bun, 'is that this is a right crock of penguins' pap!'

'You have no idea how right you are, Master Smith,' laughed the three of us.

'Listen, Bun,' I smiled, taking a seat next to him on the wall, 'perhaps the rules were shifted slightly towards a Durkin victory, but then again, perhaps they weren't. What can I say? You know boxing is fraught with politics. Come with us to Master Henton's and all will become clear.'

On the way, we stopped off at Micky F's. He appeared at the door, sporting an outstanding shiner.

'What's up, lads?' enquired our flat-headed buddy.

'Come with us, Mick,' we said. 'We've found a rightful rival for Henton's crown.'

'Who's that? Hey, wait a second. I'm not putting them flipping gloves on again.'

'No,' I said, pointing at Spinx. 'Our golden boy is standing right here. Just put your shoes on and come with us.'

Thirty-four seconds later, the five of us, with bruised faces and busted lips, were standing outside the champ's humble abode, ringing the bell. Henton swung open the door; he was wearing only his boxer shorts.

'What now?' asked the King of Sting, sucking on an ice-lolly pop.

'What now? I'll tell you what now, Mr Balboa,' I quipped. 'Okay, Dave, we understand you refuse to defend your title against any would-be challengers. Is this true?'

'That is correct,' laughed Mr H.

'Fine. Then you won't mind handing over the Championship belt, will you?' I grinned, expecting a harsh response.

'Ahey, nee bother,' chuckled Henton, heading into his lounge to retrieve the greatest prize in sport. 'Catch you later, lads. Dying for a dump!'

With that, he threw the IBF rip-off onto the lawn and slammed the door. The five of us stood there, totally speechless.

'Well, bugger my steamboat,' I smiled, picking up the belt. 'Hey, Pops, pass me that milk crate.'

Throwing the empty bottles onto Dave's lawn, Popeye handed over the crate, just as the former champ came back into view at the window.

'Thought I'd have to go the distance with him at least,' said Spinx, humbly.

Standing him on the upturned milk crate, I took the belt and fastened it firmly round his waist with a snap.

'Ladies and gents, please can I have your attention?' I continued, looking up at my bewildered pal. 'Will you all now put your hands together for... the New Heavyweight Champion of Cowgate, Mr Paul "Lights out" Durkin!'

While I and the rest of the lads jumped around in the garden like a pack of thirsty hyenas, Davie H shook his head in disbelief. Durkin punched the air and screamed,

'Yo, Adrian. I… did… it!'

And a legend was born.

Two days later, our mid-term break was over and we headed back to school. The flashes of Paul's victory, against the odds, were still ringing fresh in our minds. By morning recess, the news of Durk's magic feats in the ring was the talk of the school. By 11 o'clock, the list of casualties who had, supposedly, met his fist of doom, hovered close to the fifty mark. By lunchtime, it was 108.

'Hey, Davis, this is getting ridiculous,' cursed Durk, as we sat opposite Carrick's Bakery on Ponteland Road, eating our 27p mega-deal cream buns. 'I only had three frigging bouts and these guys think I'm the new Clubber Lang.'

'Yeah, I hear you, bud,' I agreed. 'I may have told a few people that you took out Mr H in the second round of the title decider, with an eight point combination. Apart from that, I've barely mentioned it.'

'You said what? Nee wonder all the rogues keep winking at me, like I'm the man.'

'Well, excuse me! I was only trying to hype up the fact that you're the new-found King of Cowgate.'

Spinx stormed off, launching his cream bun over his shoulder as he went.

'Nee more, Davis. Terry bleeding Boakes will be asking me to step outside pretty soon, if this goes any further..'

I suppose Durk did have a point. The last thing he needed was the likes of Terry Boakes, (the daddy in our year), throwing left crosses at his chops.

Ha, I recall the news even got back to Henton, who went to a different school, a good mile up the hill in Kenton. Some minger had stopped him on his way to class and asked him if it was true that some skinny kid from Blakelaw had burst his lips wide open in the second. No joke, that happened.

To be fair, the hype did subside after a week or so and good old Durk got by, mainly unscathed. Actually, I believe he was chased home only three or four times.

A day or two later, I received a disturbing phone call from my dad. It went like this.

'Neil, Dad here. I've had some kid from up my street here three times, looking for his boxing gloves. He says you took them over three weeks ago. You haven't seen them have you, son?'

'Er, well, you could say that, chef.'

Chapter 8

Meet Hoppy

PAUL: At the end of my street were two semi-detached houses. They were occupied by the Smyths, (whom you have met), on the left and the Hopson family on the right. They were by far the biggest houses on the street and their front windows jutted out, increasing the impression. Mark Hopson, known as "Hoppy" to the lads, would eventually become one of our friends through our terrorising his family and causing them all sorts of grief. It was always harmless fun and nothing we did ever put the family's lives in danger.

The closest we came was when Popeye threw a milk crate through the Hopsons' living room window, while they were watching "Catchphrase" one Saturday evening. I can remember it vividly. We had made a makeshift den in Hoppy's back garden and we would congregate there occasionally, to play cards or just hang out. This particular Saturday night we had knocked on Mark to come out.

'I'm watching Knightrider then Catchphrase,' said Hoppy.

'Okay,' replied John. 'Is it all right if we go round the back?'

'Aye, but keep the noise down. Me mother is having her tea,' warned Hoppy as he went back inside and shut the door.

Neil, Pops, John and I headed around the side of the Hopson house and towards the back garden. The kitchen window was on that side of the house, so we all had a gaze in as we passed. Sue (Mark's mum), Sharon and Tracey (his sisters) and Mark were all perched on the sofa, tucking into their egg and chips, and waiting eagerly for Roy Walker to chirp up with his famous "Catchphrase" saying, "Say what you see!"

We made our way to the den and clambered inside. We had managed to pick up some old carpet for the floor and taken some milk crates from the local dairy to use as seats. The four of us sat there for a while, chatting and telling jokes. Not wanting to get into trouble, Hoppy had failed to tell his mother that we were sitting in their back garden. He was hoping we'd get bored then move on. He was half right, as we did start to get a little bored.

'Fancy watching "Catchphrase" in Hoppy's house?' asked Pops.

'Aye, but his mother wouldn't let the four of us in,' replied Neil.

But Pops had an idea.

Mark's living room was at the rear of the property, so all we had to do was sneak up to the window and glance through, to watch the country's favourite game show. It did not occur to us to just go home and watch in the comfort of our own houses. John approached the living room window and peeked in. We all stood at about 5'4", so weren't the tallest kids in the world. John went onto his tiptoes but was clearly struggling.

'I can only see the top of Roy's head,' he said.

'What are the others doing?' asked Neil.

'Just chilling out, enjoying TV by the look of things,' replied John.

I joined him, standing on tiptoe and peered into the Hopson living room. Mark, Tracey and Sharon were snuggled up on the couch, while Sue lazed in a chair, her feet propped up on the small coffee table.

'Here, lads, catch this,' said Pops.

I turned to see a milk crate flying towards my face. I managed to push John out of the way and ducked at the same time. The crate sailed over my head and straight through the Hopsons' living room window.

'Whoops!' came the shout from Pops.

We heard the sound of glass smash as it hit the floor of the living room, then screams pierced our ears as Mark and his family started yelling and cursing. The four of us darted from the garden, ducking as we passed the kitchen window. We sprinted as fast as we could up the street, not stopping until we reached the Blue Door. We were all out of breath as we came to a stop. I looked at John, John looked at Neil, then we all stared at Pops.

'What?' he asked, with a quizzical look on his face.

We all burst out laughing, shaking our heads at the same time. I glanced at John, who had tears streaming down his face. None of us could speak for a minute or so. Finally, we regained some composure and tried to take in what had just happened.

'I spotted you on your tiptoes, Chuck, so I decided to throw you a crate to stand on,' said Pops. 'I must have hoyed it too hard.'

'That's an understatement,' I commented.

'I hope they didn't see us or I'm ganna be in some bother with me fatha,' added Jay.

Jason's father, Raymond, was a no-nonsense man, who cracked you across the earhole first and asked questions later. I knew the rest of us would also be in trouble if we were discovered to have been at the scene of the incident. We were all apprehensive about going back down the street, even though our curiosity was killing us. We sat for about ten minutes before a small, thin figure appeared from around the corner of the dairy.

'Who did that?' shouted Hoppy, clearly in a rage. 'Who did it?' he repeated to himself.

He looked like he was foaming at the mouth as he approached us

'Hoppy, just calm down,' said Neil, trying to diffuse the situation.

'Calm down? Calm down? A milk crate has just nearly chopped me mam's heed off!'

'Have you grassed on us?' asked Pops.

'I can't,' replied Hoppy. 'If I told me mother that I let you round the back, she'd take me heed off. That doesn't hide the fact that someone has just thrown a crate through me sitting room window.'

'Okay, Hoppy,' said Pops, 'it was... Paul.'

'You lying sod, Pops. It wasn't me, it was... him,' I replied, pointing at Pops , who was now grinning like a Cheshire cat.

'Oh, sorry, come to think of it now, it was… John.'

'Eh?' said John. 'I could have sworn it was… Neil.'

Hoppy's face looked a tad confused as we all continued to blame each other.

'Stop messing on and tell me who done it,' he shouted at us.

'The fact is, we can't remember, Hoppy. It may not even have been one of us, if the truth be known,' answered John.

'Well, me mother's called the busies [police] and they'll want a name,' replied Hoppy.

'We'll just tell them you let us go into the back garden. We were there by consent,' said Neil.

Hoppy's face turned to thunder and he marched off.

'You bunch of swines. I'll get you all back some time.'

We watched him trudge off and disappear round the corner.

'Nice one, Pops,' I said. 'Thought you were trying to finger me with the blame.'

'I was!' said Pops.

Hoppy managed to keep his mouth shut and Sue never found out who put a Co-operative milk crate through her living room window. The police left a number, in case any more details came to light, and the council's emergency joiner boarded up the window until a new pane of glass could be fitted. It was just another typical night in Whitethorn Crescent.

Another occasion which springs to mind is the time when the Hopson house turned white, owing to the number of snowballs we threw at it. At one point, fifteen people were making and throwing snowballs at the font of the house. All the family protested and told us to stop, but that didn't deter us. They would usually end up with a snowball being pelted off their head. If I remember correctly, two windows were smashed that day. This resulted in the Hopsons' getting reinforced glass in every window on the property.

I also remember Pops stacking up several milk crates against the front door, ringing the bell and running away. We would peer over the fence to see Hoppy open the door and a pile of crates fall on top of him. This was harmless fun and Hoppy seemed to take it as a joke.

On yet another occasion, Pops could, I suppose, have been arrested for breaking and entering. He was desperate for the toilet and, rather than walk the short distance home, he decided to scale the external drainpipe on the rear of the Hopson house. We had congregated in Hoppy's back garden again for a spot of socialising. Hoppy himself had gone into the house some ten minutes earlier and had not reappeared.

'I need to send the brown trout downstream,' Pops said, grimacing because of stomach cramps.

'If you run, you may not follow through,' I commented.

'I've a better idea. Keep toot [lookout],' answered Popeye.

He headed for the drainpipe and, with the ease of a young Peter Parker, started to climb up the wall. He reached the top and, to his left, the bathroom window stood open. We watched as he grabbed the window ledge and bundled his way through the small opening. Neil and I started to laugh. We couldn't believe he would have the balls to do such a thing. Then again, we knew never to underestimate Popeye. After a few moments, we heard a commotion from the bathroom, then shouting. About a minute later, Pops appeared from the house with a grin as wide as the Tyne.

'How did you get in that way, then come out by the front door?' I asked.

'Well,' he said, 'after getting through the window, I immediately located the bog and made a dart for it. I pulled down my pants and released the chocolate hostage. In my state of panic, I failed to realise the bath was in use.'

Pops had sat on the toilet to let nature take its course, but had not seen the body submerged in the tub. As the critical moment approached, Mark Hopson suddenly sprang up from the bubbles to see Popeye's distorted face as he battled with nature's flushable gift. He was only three feet from where the man of the house had been enjoying his tranquil dip.

'What the flippin' heck are you doing?' screamed Mark.

'Taking a dump. What does it look like?' replied Pops, calmly.

'How did you get in? Get out of my house!' yelled the naked Hoppy.

'Calm doon, cho. I'm just in the process of wiping me jacksy,' answered Pops.

'Mark! Mark!' screamed a very agitated Mrs Hopson from the other side of the locked door.

Pops stood up and unlocked the door. Sue Hopson fell into the bathroom, bewildered by the sight before him. Pops gave her a sly wink as he departed from the establishment.

'I would spray some air freshener before you go in there, pet. It bloody stinks,' he said as he continued down the stairs and out via the front door.

We walked along and sat on my step. Hoppy arrived about twenty minutes later, still reeling from his bathroom experience.

'Can't believe you done that, Popeye,' he said 'How did you get into my house? The bathroom door was locked and I'm sure I shut the window.'

'I'm a master of illusion,' answered Pops. 'Paul Daniels can only do card tricks, whereas I can pass through walls!'

Hoppy looked as his mother had, earlier. Sue never phoned the police, so Pops was off the hook.

I don't think Pops ever told Hoppy how he got into the bathroom that day. Hoppy often asked but Pops and I would not be surprised if he still thinks about it.

Stepfather

NEIL: Back then in Cowgate, it wasn't just the beatings or the threats; no, petty crime circled and swayed through our streets like some rotting river with burnt out cars for shark fins. All my pals had been robbed or knew someone who had been. Even if you had not been, you would say you had, if some posh chap from Dallas Hall asked you. In a way, a shallow way, it was cool to be surrounded by all that criminal activity. Some of the girls at school thought you were a bit of a rebel. And the others? Well, they just thought you were a bamp.

As much as I would like to condemn the place and wish it ill, I cannot. Those streets and the majority of the characters who walked them were okay. If they knew you, they usually liked you. I have no idea why our tight group of lads were not out there, nicking people's cars or their other worldly treasures. Seriously, we were no angels, but hey, then again we were no bastards either.

For me personally, growing up as a kid was a crazy thing. At times between the walls of my council house there was an unforgettable roller-coaster ride waiting – often guaranteed – to happen.

I recall with unease when I was eleven years old and my dear momma's second marriage was in full swing. It had been a good two years since my dad had headed away to his tiny rented bed-sit, which had only enough space for one single bed and no cats. Only two years! Even at that age, I knew inside that without him, I was lost. My new step-dad had not taken long to settle in and feel at home. I think it had taken only six or seven months for him to let loose his monsters on his new brood of three with his fists and feet. Yes, it hadn't taken long at all, before he had every one of us blinded and paralysed by fear. Whether he was throwing armchairs through glass tables or hurling new-born puppies in the air, he was rarely still long enough to really comprehend what damage he was doing to us all, never mind why.

To be fair to my mother, in my eyes she held little blame for this shiny new evil that had landed upon us. How was she to know that her brand new Mr Right was anything but? You had to give him his due; this lump of lard was not just pig ugly and fat, the guy was very clever too. He knew fine and well that, for a while, he would have to make all the right noises. Like, say, when the 11-year-old son of his intended wanted to show him round his bedroom collection of Star Wars toys, or his outstanding Subbuteo soccer memorabilia, it was, 'Oh, Neil, these toys are great!'

However, before the ink had dried on the wedding certificate, it was Boooom!

'Children... daddy's home!'

I think it was some three or four weeks after first meeting him that my concerns had begun to arise. We were just sitting there, having an innocent conversation about nothing in particular, when the topic changed to women. Like thunder, his mood went as black as his eyes.

'You should be careful of them,' he said, through gritted teeth and flaring his nostrils. 'They're nothing but trouble.'

'Who are?' I croaked back, fearing his rage.

'All of them,' he finished, standing up. 'All of them.'

Next door in the kitchen, my mum prepared dinner, blissfully unaware of our little chat.

The alarm bells rang fresh in my brain. I just thanked the Lord and counted my blessings that, with Christmas fast approaching, I had not shared with the fat toad the hope that I might get a bike. For Mr Step-dad here, it seemed as though he was on some kind of valuable mission. It was perfectly plain and painfully obvious to me and my big sister Michelle that this guy was out to destroy our lives. Looking back to those long troubling times, I still feel his eyes in every single corner of our modest three-bedroomed terraced council house. Now, however, one thing has changed. These days, that shaking, feeble little boy, who dreamt of the day when he might protect both his dear mother and sister from the abuse and blows, is definitely no longer scared.

'Six feet high and six feet wide.' These were the mortal and cruel words that he used to whisper in my ear as he grimaced and terrorised us. 'You can grow six feet high and six feet wide, and you'll never be able to stop me,' he raged, towering over a shaking child with his venom and shifting fat. How brave and powerful you must have felt, Step-daddy!

For me, every child out there who shares a smile has a story. Even now, a good twenty years on, I still know very little of what went on behind those hidden walls of my closest friends and life-long brothers. Though, looking back and looking forward, I know that for this kid, now a father himself, one thing is certain. Behind my walls and locked doors, for many years there lay a monster… there lay a monster.

Chapter 9

Wayne Aldred

PAUL: Wayne Aldred… Where do I start? A couple of years after knocking about with the gang, I was introduced to Wayne by John Ingram. His mother lived in close proximity to the Blue Door, but he only visited during school holidays, as his parents were separated. Wayne had a Yorkshire accent, coming from Halifax, and he brought with him a swagger and presence like nothing the other lads had seen before. Admittedly, he was good-looking, 5'11", with a good physique. The downside to this was that he knew it! The phrase, "I think she fancies me,' when liaising with the opposite sex, was frequently used if Wayne was around. The only thing that let him down was his Rick Astley-type haircut. He had a quiff which the most hardened Teddy-boy would have been proud of. Wayne was a couple of years older than us and was a man of the world, if you get my meaning. We would all listen intently to stories of "ham shanks" and "blow jobs". I shall be forever in his debt for introducing us to rap music, such as the Beastie Boys and Run DMC. Later on it progressed to NWA and Easy E, which shocked us at first. However, we soon got used to the violent and sexual lyrical content.

Wayne also thought of himself as a "boy from the 'hood," having introduced us to rap music. He had developed the notion that he could sign-write and "tag". I remember vividly one occasion, when he led us down the subways with a couple of cans of spray paint which he had managed to whip from his step-dad's garage. One was silver and the other a violent shade of maroon (like his dad's Vauxhall Cavalier Estate).

'Stand back, boys, and watch the magic happen,' said Wayne, nodding his head while I looked slightly perplexed.

He went to work on the white-washed subway wall, shaking the can vigorously every so often. I asked a couple of times what he was actually drawing, but he just replied with a mumble and carried on spraying. Ten minutes later, he stood back to admire his work.

'What do you think, eh?' asked Wayne, with a smile as wide as the Tyne.

'Why would you draw a turtle?' replied Neil.

'Turtle? Turtle? You cheeky git!' hissed Wayne. 'It's a flippin' Adidas symbol.'

It took a few minutes to figure this out, but after a few manoeuvres with our heads, the sign became clear.

'I hope you're not going into design when you leave school,' said Henton. 'That must be the worst Adidas sign I've ever seen.'

'You Geordie boys wouldn't know the art of spray painting if it came up and bit you on the backside,' said Wayne, rather smugly.

He tried his hand at other murals and, to be fair, they were a lot better than our efforts. I came out of school with a GCSE Grade E for Art and Design; from this, you can tell what rubbish I used to draw. Wayne was by no means a Picasso, but he gave it his best.

Kill the fox

NEIL: It's accurate to say that we all liked Wayne from the beginning. For starters, he was huge, compared to us weasels. He was a right good-looking git too, and boy, did he know it! You bet your Wonder Woman T-shirt he did. And once Mr Aldred had settled into the manor, no lady in sunny Cowgate was safe.

Wayne was, of course, also brilliant at everything. Then again, football was not his forte; he played as though his feet were knotted together. (Southerners, eh?)

I remember with horror how, one time, we had to rip up the rule book of Kill the Fox, a game in which one team is the fox, the other team the hunter. The basic concept was simple. The team of foxes had five minutes to run like the wind, then the hunters would give chase and bring them down by any means possible. And yes, I mean any. Hence the name of the game, which at a later date was re-named Batter the Fox.

As you can imagine, once the boy wonder arrived with his dashing horse speed and flying shovel fists, a pleasant one-hour game of blood and carnage was now over in mere minutes. After much deliberation, he did take the news very well that, for the remainder of his stay within the confines of the sunny north-east, he would only be allowed to be a fluffy fox.

Oh – did we mention that he was pants at football?

Welcome to Gosforth

NEIL: During another time of stupidity, in the late summer of 1986, our loyalties had, for a time, switched from the unsafe streets of Costa del Cowgate. By a majority vote, we relocated to the posh end of town, Gosforth. Gossie was where all the high society folk tended to fine dine with chums over a calm cognac, by a log fire in some marvellous hotel piano lounge. Yes, you could certainly find the money in Gossie. Here lived the City's top brass, such as doctors and politicians. Naturally, many of the local Pakistani mini-mart owners resided here too.

One evening, I, Popeye, Henton, Ingram, Durk, Micky F and, last but not least, our nasal chum Bun, found ourselves deep within a thicket inside some rich folk's one acre back garden.

'Okay, lads,' began Squadron Leader Ingram, 'we all know why we're here tonight, don't we?'

'I frigging don't' replied Micky F who, like the rest of us, was kitted out all in black, face smeared with mud.

'Excuse me!' shrieked John, causing the rest of us to giggle uncontrollably behind the safety of a perfect line of 12-foot ferns which formed a protective divide from the main lawn and garden.

Once again, like many of our peculiar projects, the concept of our being huddled together, dressed as Ninjas, in some stranger's rear garden, was pretty straightforward. Popeye and Bun had come up with a revolutionary new plan. Basically, we were to get from one end of Gosforth to the other by crossing other people's back gardens, fences and sheds. On paper, the project was a breeze. However, this was summer time and people were outside, enjoying the early evening weather – in their own gardens too! It seemed that the chances of our carrying out our simple task, without being attacked by disapproving hounds and boozed-up neighbours, hung somewhat in the balance.

'Okay,' continued Ingram. 'If we stick to the bushes, we should meet no resistance. And if you care to look west, you will notice the light is fading fast.'

'Let's do it!' we chimed in unison, as we set off across a pristine lawn and over a 5-foot fence.

'Remember,' added Popeye, 'if a demented pooch comes after you, you have the trees. I've never met a dog yet who could negotiate a flippin' birch.'

'Cujo could,' smiled Flappy, as we darted across the next garden's lawn via a 7-foot fluffy hedge, chuckling our asses off.

After about an hour, half our task was completed. We waited patiently behind a rose bush for Micky F, who was still stuck in the previous garden. He was trying to pluck up the courage to jump out of some kid's feeble tree-house and use a rather impressive 12-foot tree fern as a brake, as the rest of us had just done.

'For the love of God, will you hurry up,' pleaded Henton. 'Just jump.'

At last, our flat-headed friend came crashing over the trees landing with a thump, and we proceeded to move on into the darkness. As we were about to break through the cover of the bushes, Henton paused.

'Sshhh,' he said. 'There's something happening through here. I can see lights.'

Dropping to our knees like the soldiers we weren't, we halted momentarily under the bushes, to see what was happening at the bottom of the cruise-ship-sized garden.

'Well, bugger me sideways,' exclaimed Popeye in disgust. 'The gypoes are only having an outdoor banquet.'

'Ahey, and what's wrong with that?' considered Micky .

'The swines never sent my invite. That's what's wrong,' tutted Pops, heading down the lawn to join the guests.

'Unbelievable!' laughed Ingram, rubbing his eyes.

'Ahey, the crazy bugger's got some balls,' said Durkin proudly, as some forty feet away, our dear chum had somehow managed to blend in perfectly among the guests and was proceeding towards the buffet table to get himself a plate.

'I've seen it all now,' laughed Fox. 'I've seen it frigging all!'
After another ten minutes, while we waited and wondered what to do next, Davie Henton, who had crawled unseen down the side of the garden, suddenly rose to his feet. He joined Pops, who was with a dentist, in deep conversation about his dear mother's cavities.

'This is ridiculous,' snapped Bun, as we lay on our stomachs under the privet. 'Here we are, playing Hamburger-flipping-Hill and those two gits are down there, eating cake.'
Our eyes met and Durkin rose to his knees.

'Hey, to hell with this. Bun's right. Come on, lads, let's dine!'
Later, with our stomachs content, we took the short cut home across the moors, filling the night with our laughter.

'Nice folks,' we agreed, as we headed back into Cowgate.

'Hmm, yes,' chuckled Popeye. 'I really must send them a thank you card and congratulate them on that splendid hock!'

Chapter 10

For my Gran

PAUL: I explained earlier that when we Durkins' moved back to Cowgate in October 1980, it was for all the right reasons. My mother was not happy where we lived and her place of employment was in Cowgate. Most importantly, my elderly grandparents resided there. I was very close to my grandma and would sleep five out of seven nights a week at her house. She was a very kind woman, who would give you her last penny. At the ripe old age of 74, she would still meet friends in the local pub, the Ord Arms, and sit reminiscing about days gone by. It was a rough pub, with a bad reputation, but when I was allowed, I would sometimes join her (me with a Coke) in the snug, a small room at the rear of the bar, big enough for about ten people. On one occasion, during my Adam and the Ants phase, I played "Stand and Deliver" about thirty times on the jukebox. The locals were not happy; I can still picture their faces…

'If I hear "da diddley qua qua, da diddley qua qua" once more, I'm going to launch that bloody jukebox out the window!' bawled one of the regulars.

I have another vivid memory of spending nearly all of the six-week summer holiday at my gran's house, circa 1983. There was the same ritual every morning: bowl of porridge, then back to bed. I would catch the end of Mad Lizzie doing her work-out with some puffed-out celebrity, to King Creole and the Sunshine Band's "Give it Up". Following that, I would watch Roland Rat and Kevin the Gerbil for half an hour, before the Adventures of Huckleberry Finn rounded off my morning viewing. I wouldn't get out of bed before 10.30am.

My grandparents lived only a short walk from my house, in a ground floor flat. Gran had suffered with angina for several years and Granddad's health was never the best. He used to smoke roll-up cigarettes and I cannot recall ever seeing him without one in his nicotine-stained fingers. This was to catch up with him finally and in March 1984 lung cancer was diagnosed. He managed to survive for three months before losing the battle on 9th June. Although they had not seen eye to eye for some time, my grandparents had been married for over fifty years, so the loss came as a terrible blow to Gran. I was sitting on her bed when one of my aunties came and told me that Granddad had just died. This wave of sadness came across me. I felt numb inside. It was my first experience of death and I started to weep into my hands.

The weeks following my granddad's death are a blur, really. I can recall my gran's not wanting to stay in the flat any longer, because of the painful memories. My mother petitioned the local council office, to try and get her a move. (She had an extra bit of clout as she worked there as a cleaner.) Within six weeks, the council had found Gran a new residence, but it was a house rather than a flat, which she would have preferred.

It took literally thirty seconds to get from our house to Gran's new one, on Chestnut Avenue. Everyone was happy and we helped her to move into the house in late August 1984. After a few weeks, it became apparent that she was struggling to cope with the flight of stairs and so my Uncle Johnny gave up his own flat to move in with her. He was a great help and Gran felt more secure having him there.

Friday 30th November was a cold, wet, miserable day. I had slept at my gran's house the previous night, to keep her company. I had ironed my school kit and placed it on the end of the bed for the following morning. I was asleep on my small camp-bed when, around 4.30am, the main light in the room was switched on. I stirred and sat up in bed. My gran was sitting on the edge of her bed, wheezing heavily.

'Are you okay, Grandma?' I asked.

'I'm fine, love. Just finding it a bit hard to get my breath, that's all. Go back to sleep; you've got to be up in three hours, for school,' she answered.

I laid my head down on the pillow, looking in her direction. She stood up after a short while and propped up the pillows before climbing back into bed. She then opened her bottle of angina pills and placed one under her tongue.

'Are you not asleep yet?' she asked.

I said I was worried about her but she assured me she was all right. Honest. She wheezed for a few seconds more, then reached out and grabbed me tightly around the wrist. There was a look of panic on her face.

'Paul, get Johnny. Quick!' she called out.

My gran then clutched at her nightdress and started to fall sideways out of the bed. I screamed and ran to the top of the stairs, squealing Johnny's name. He slept on the sofa most nights and on this occasion had been woken by a thump. Without hesitating, he bolted up the stairs, taking two at a time, and ran to the corner of the room, where my gran was now slumped. He picked her up and cradled her in his arms.

'Get home and call 999,' Johnny yelled at me. Unfortunately, my gran did not have a land line telephone and mobiles were still, in 1984, an item of science fiction, so I had to run round to my house to call for an ambulance. I sprinted the short distance as fast as possible. The wind and rain were pounding against my face as I dashed through the garden gate and banged on the door. Tears were streaming down my face when my mother opened the door, perplexed and dazed.

'Me grandma, me grandma,' I screamed at my mother, 'she's collapsed and Johnny's with her. I need to phone an ambulance!'

I can vaguely remember my mother crying, "Oh no, oh no," over and over again, while she was throwing on a jumper and a pair of jeans. She left the house in a panic and it was down to me to phone for the ambulance. I dialled 999 and gave the details of what had happened. When the operator asked for the address, I had a mental block and gave my address in error. Just then, Johnny burst into the room, shouting. He wanted to know when the ambulance would be with us.

'I'm calling them now,' I yelled back at him.

'Hurry up!' he screeched. 'You've been gone five minutes and still haven't rung for the ambulance.'

'What's me grandma's address? I've forgotten,' I called.

At this point, Johnny snatched the phone from my hand and started talking to the operator. The call ended within thirty seconds and Johnny slumped on my mother's bed and gave out a large sigh.

'I'm sorry, I'm sorry,' I cried as tears ran down my cheeks.

'She's gone, Paul,' Johnny said in a low voice. He looked down at the floor and then at me.

'Don't say that!' I screamed at him. 'Don't you say that!'

The ambulance arrived in no time. Johnny and I got back to my gran's just as she was being transported from the house into the vehicle. My mother climbed into the back of the ambulance and it sped off. Johnny and I watched the flashing light fade into the distance.

Around 6.00am we received a call from the hospital, saying Gran had died. She had had a massive heart attack and, no matter how fast the ambulance had been, it would have done no good. She had died in Johnny's arms that morning. We all knew, but didn't want to admit it to ourselves.

I had the terrible task of going with Johnny to other relatives, to tell them the awful news. My mother was still at the hospital, now with one of my cousins, dealing with the necessary paperwork. We visited three of my aunties before 9 o'clock that morning, each with the same reaction. I found I would stop crying but, as soon as I entered another relative's home, the waterworks would start again and I would sob uncontrollably. During all of this, Johnny kept a level head and did not shed a tear. I think he stayed strong for me and, to this day, I am grateful to him for that.

Gran's funeral took place exactly a week later, on the Friday. I am unsure what time it took place, but it was during my school lunch hour. I walked to the top of the road and sat in a bus shelter. I knew the hearse had to pass here, on its way to the crematorium, so I was hoping to catch one last glimpse of my gran. A couple of days earlier my mother had asked whether I wanted to attend the funeral, but I thought I had done all the crying I could do. I therefore passed up the offer and decided to go to school, to try to keep my mind occupied.

The hearse did not pass in the hour I sat at the bus stop with my head in my hands, so I pulled myself to my feet and trudged back to school. All afternoon I had an empty feeling in the pit of my stomach, and I was in my own world during the remainder of the day's lessons.

I heard from relatives that the funeral went as well as expected and my gran got a good turn out. Uncle Johnny took her death the worst out of all the family. He became a recluse in the months that followed, culminating in his having a nervous breakdown. The family helped him through this but I do not think that, even after twenty-two years, he has ever fully recovered from the loss.

My mother also took Gran's death really hard. She could not deal with the loss of her mother and I believe that, to this day, she has visited the grave only once. Some people may say this is disrespectful and uncaring, but this is how my mother has coped with it. She feels she does not need to visit the crematorium to remember Gran.

I try to think of my gran as the happy-go-lucky person she was. She had time for everyone and I know that I'm a better person for spending time with her.

Blaydon FC

NEIL: September 1989 was to be the year when my own particular football career reached its height. When I say height, I mean the time it seemed to be almost perfect. And no, sadly, it hadn't a thing to do with the sweet Toon Army either. In fact, a local side known as Blaydon Town

FC had stolen my heart.

Back then, playing at Blaydon was beyond class. The main reason had nothing to do with football, because, in truth, we were worse than pants. Okay, pants may be slightly harsh, but hey, we were never quite your Real Madrid.

It was Scotty Fenton, from the Rothbury camping trip, (more later...), who had introduced me to this soccer heaven just south of the river. I recall with glee our very first game of the season. With only moments to go before the final whistle, we were trailing 9-0, when at last my true defining moment came to pass. The referee had his whistle in his mouth when I took advantage of a simple defensive error and burst an unstoppable low drive into the corner of the net. Racing away with venom, I punched the air in delight as the ref blew final time.

Back in the changing room, while our manager went ape, I re-played my Van Basten-like strike over and over again in my young mind.

'...And what in the flying **** are you so happy about, Mr Davis?' enquired Alan, our flustered coach.

'Oh, I'm just chuffed to bits, Alan. Yee naa, being top scorer and that,' I quipped, feeling invincible.

I shared my smirk with my homeboy Durkin, who had also signed his life away on the dotted line, albeit in the name of his younger cousin, one Lee Chamberlain. I should explain that our dear Durk was, at seventeen, a little too old to play in our team. Not that our manager ever found out; a dodgy birth certificate was obtained somehow from the kind staff at our local Civic Centre.By the time of our much anticipated second league fixture, away to Clara Vale FC, we had managed to recruit another three members from our own Cowgate mean street band. They were one Popeye/Coco Allison (left back), Master Bun Smith (left wing) and John/Chuck Berry Ingram (midfield general).

At the end of ninety minutes, we mere mortals had tasted glory. Coming out 4-2 winners, with a brace from yours truly, a wonder strike from our versatile right back, Master Flappy Durkin, and a neat tap in at the far post by some other striker, we were now well on our way. With three points sweetly on the board, after two matches we found ourselves amazingly in sixth spot.

'Divent naa aboot yees,' chimed young Pops after a long choke on his McDonald's strawberry milkshake.

'Don't know aboot what?' enquired Ingram, with a shrug, as we sat comfortably in our favourite eatery at the top end of Newcastle's Northumberland Street.

Pops continued nosing through the sports pages of our local rag the Evening Chronicle.

'Looking at these league tables, I'd say that with two more wins, the frigging title could be ours.'

'Eh?' shrieked Ingram, spraying young Bun with a mouthful of warm apple pie. 'Title? Ours? We've only played two freaking games, you glakey git!'

Unmoved, Popeye pointed at our position in the table and smiled.

'The league doesn't lie, my Chuck-berried friend, the league does not lie.'

Some ten games later, with a tally of eleven points firmly on the scoreboard, we found ourselves sitting snugly at fourth from bottom!

'You frigging cabbage,' Ingram sneered fondly at Pops, after checking our weekly standings.

However, one thing we managed to win every week was the team's weekly money draw. Yet again, this was achieved through a cunning plan. It seemed we had come up with an easy but productive way of never losing when it came to the once-a-week number lottery. As I'm sure you have guessed by now, our devious scam to con our other team-mates out of their hard earned cash was so simple and obvious that it was near on perfect. At the draw, one person had to dip his hand into a bag, pick out a numbered ball and call out the lucky winner. Simple, right? Wrong, hee hee!

There were always at least four of our crowd in the team, who, by the way, were mostly hated by the rest of the Blaydon contingent, basically because we came from Cowgate. There would be a few of us around on draw day, so we made sure it was one of us who picked out the lucky number. Of course, we all knew one another's numbers by heart, so all we needed to do was pull out a ball, shout out one of our own numbers and throw the true winning number back into the bag before anyone could contest it. Meanwhile, as the other tossers scratched their heads in disbelief that those jammy swines from Cow-frigging-gate had won again, we fine men from the manor chased each other around the gymnasium in a state of utter glee. Once again, like every other week, a McDonald's Happy Meal for four was briskly secured!

Incredible as it seems, not once did any of those dizzy buggers ever try to say that we had cheated. On one occasion I did actually pick out my own flipping number and, as the others stood there, shaking their heads, I just froze, unable to comprehend what I should do next. As the games kept coming in thick and fast, so did the milkshakes.

I don't think we managed, all season long, to get out of the bottom half of the table. Not that we lads minded; like with everything else, we were only there for the food and the crack.

I suppose my truly finest hour was when I managed to notch up five goals in one game. With only moments to go before the final whistle, the game was tied at 5-5 and it seemed that my place in Blaydon schoolboy soccer history would be set in stone. That was until a very young Popeye Allison decided to give away two late injury-time penalties and we came away having lost 7-5. Even so, the Evening Chronicle did award me a cracking headline in their Thursday edition. It read: "Davis hits five! But hapless Blaydon still lose." After this, it was official – I was now a god!

Another great aspect of applying our talents to Blaydon FC was the fact that, for some reason, we always attracted a fine, loyal following crowd. Yes, come rain or shine, it was not unheard of for twenty to thirty ladies and gents to come and show their support. More importantly, they would remind us, with their wild bellowing and waving fists, just how utterly terrible they believed we were.

I recall fondly one chubby young fellow who really stood out more. A bloke no older than us, at sweet fifteen, Minto was without doubt our most loyal and diehard fan. All of us Cowgate lads had taken to Minto straight away. He shared our stupid sense of humour and, from the beginning, he seemed to grasp what we were all about. To our eyes, this was a refreshing change from the cold shoulder that we usually got from the Blaydon boys.

In all my time there, bursting the net for Blaydon, our new chum Minto never missed a match. We could have been playing against a Gobi Desert eleven and that chubby bugger would have been there on the back of a camel. What a kid he was; a true gem and a gent.

Sadly, this brings me swiftly on to one of the most outrageous and hilarious scenes I have ever witnessed. It all happened, like most funny things, by accident. I wonder, would you believe that a certain Master Jason/Popeye/Coco Allison was involved in this moment of mayhem?

One of our games was coming to a close, with some fifteen minutes remaining, when our coach gave Popeye the thumbs up and signalled that he should get himself warmed up.

'Minto!' chirped Pops, standing about 20 feet away, on the sideline.

'Minto, come on, mate, let's pass the ball up to one another. I'm ganning on in a minute,'

They kicked the ball back and forth for a while, then Popeye upped the tempo with a couple of quick whizzing passes up the line to young Mints. Suddenly, after trapping the ball with his foot, Popeye passed it back towards his chubby chum and started running at speed in his direction. Taking the pass with ease, Minto looked up to see a hurtling Popeye sliding towards him on his backside in a two-footed tackle.

The next thing we saw from our vantage point on the pitch was dear Pops, crashing feet first into a bewildered Minto, who was by now halfway through his second triple salko somersault. Pretty soon the game was declared void, cancelled as the groundsmen needed to clear a path for the imminent arrival of an ambulance. I don't think my pals had ever laughed as hard in their lives, as when poor Mints was loaded into the back of that flashing four-wheeler. Later, Pops tried to humour us with pleas that Minto had taken a tumble and dived. "A' frigging swear doon," is how I think he worded it.

You had to give young Minto his dues. Come the measure of the lad, he never held a grudge, nor did he once try to contest Popeye's many pleas of innocence. And you bet, the very next weekend and home fixture, there he was, with a brand new arm-length plaster cast protecting his dislocated shoulder and shattered wrist.

As the season came to a close, I was awarded the Leading Goal-scorer's Trophy and Golden Boot, for my fine tally of twenty-one goals in twenty-one games. Much credit, I suspect, was due to the Gola football boots, kindly given to me by one Angie Hetherington, proud owner of North Shields' premier sports store, Super Sports.

Unbeknown to us fellows of the turf, the delightful shining cup would, in future, far off days, be competed for on the pristine beaches of sunny California, with a new name to boot: the Chutney Challenge Chalice.

Master Durkin, for his rock-like defensive displays at the back, was handed the hallowed Players' Player of the Year award. Unfortunately for him, it had his cousin's name on it!

Blaydon finished fourth from bottom that season. Minto never again played darts or threw a javelin with his right arm.

A big thank you goes out to all those lads of Blaydon from '89-90, even though we might not always have been welcome. Oh, how we enjoyed your company and, of course, your total inability to spot a crook!

Chapter 11

Dodgy legal advice

NEIL: A few years back, one of Spinx's younger cousins and the future founder of the Chutney movement (coming soon in our next best selling novel?…), One Master Lee "Caplottie Duck" Thornton, actually got the bullet from Macdonald's at their West Denton branch, for the slight misdemeanour of emptying the outside litter bins onto the roof of his boss's parked car after a wild night out on the pop.

His ring piece was twitching like a virgin rabbit's nose when the date for his tribunal finally came through.

'Listen, Lee,' I said, trying on the older, wiser brotherly hat for a moment. 'Listen, no matter what they say to you, just deny everything and you'll be home free.'

'I can't, man,' Lee said solemnly. 'They've got me on frigging CCTV, River Dancing on the bonnet.'

'And?' I went on, stone coldly. 'That's hardly any proof, if you ask me.'

I turned, nodding to Durkin, who held my momentum superbly with a shrug of his shoulders, as if to say, "What's the big deal?"

Later, Lee tried our tactless approach and, unfortunately, was sacked on the spot. Durk and I absolved ourselves of any blame, of course. At the end of the day, we decided, he'd been asking for it all along. We shared this valid point with him, the second he was thrown out of the building, which only battered the poor guy's head up times ten, before he stormed off in a strop.

Three weeks later, our peculiar young pal had calmed down sufficiently to be approached and he went through the repartee that had got him fired and literally thrown out.

'So there we were, sat in her office. Then Boom! they play me the bleeding tape of me dancing on the bonnet. The next thing, they freeze frame the screen, with my face clearly seen, mouthing he words "F*** you!" at the camera.'

'So what did you do next, Lee?' enquired Durk'

'Nothing. I did what you both said. I frigging denied it.'

'And then?' I followed, trying my best not to wet myself.

' And then I was ejected out of the building, like you both saw.'

'Hmmm, I don't know about you, Paul,' I winked, 'but we could have a case of unfair dismissal here.'

Finally, we lost our grip and fell to the floor in tears of laughter. With hindsight, perhaps we should have kept our noses out. After all, this was the kid's job and we had helped him lose it. I like to think, however, that we really did him a favour that day.

Work daze

PAUL: Back then, the only available work suitable for a 12 to 15-year-old, was as a paperboy or girl. Popeye had managed to get some part time work during holidays and weekends, at a bakery up in Ponteland, a small village about seven miles from Newcastle. No doubt about it, Jason was a grafter and he would do quite a few hours at this place, to earn a bit of pocket money. His sister, Susan, already worked there and she had got him the start as a casual employee. After working at the bakery for about three months, Pops approached me.

'Hey, Spinx, I've been asked off the gaffer if I know anyone who would like to do casual work. They have a couple of positions open.'

'Would you be working there?' I enquired.

'Aye, you would be doing the same shifts as me, Monday to Thursday, 7.30am until 4.30pm. You'd get around £10 a day.'

Ten pounds sounded a lot of money to a kid who had nothing. It was just over £1 an hour. Who said slave labour was dead?

'Yeah, I'll definitely start, mate. Let me know when and where,' I replied.

The second week of the summer holiday was upon us. I had to meet Popeye and Susan at 6.35am, to catch the 6.45 bus to Ponteland. I had never been up so early in my life, so this was a bit of a culture shock and I found it tough to drag myself out of bed. We reached the bakery at 7.20am and I barely had time to take off my coat before being escorted into a small packaging room.

'You'll be working in here today, son,' said the supervisor, whose name now eludes me.

I looked around to see one girl at a packaging machine; no sign of Popeye or Susan. The girl introduced herself as Andrea and showed me what I would be doing. Basically, she put bread buns into packs of twelve, they were sent down a conveyor belt and I was at the end, waiting to place them in large bread baskets. That sounded straightforward enough until the machine started. Packets of buns started spitting their way towards me faster than you could say "Hovis". I tried to pack them as fast as I could, but kept falling behind. (They had to be put in the trays in a certain way, or everything went tits up.)

After three hours, I was given a ten-minute break. My back was busting through bending and putting the buns into trays. I met Pops.

'How you getting on, dude?' he asked.

'I'm bloody knackered,' I replied. 'All I've done is put bread into big plastic containers.'

'Aye, that's where the vacancy was – packaging. I'm round the corner, actually making the buns.'

'Wish I was there,' I huffed, taking a swig of my Rola Cola.

We met again at lunchtime, after another gruelling two-hour shift. We ate outside the bakery. My mother had put me up a packed lunch of tuna sandwiches, a corned beef pastie and a peach Melba. This was washed down with what remained of my Rola Cola.

During the afternoon shift, a couple of school lads joined us in the packaging room. They had a regular part time shift after school and one of them took over from Andrea, operating the machinery. Four-thirty couldn't come fast enough for me. I just kept telling myself "ten pound, ten pound". I barely spoke a word to Susan or Popeye as we rode home to Cowgate in the No 76 bus. I think Pops asked me how my first day had gone, and I mumbled something incoherent back to him.

I staggered into the house around 5.30pm and slumped on the sofa. After a bite to eat, I set my alarm for 6.00am and went to bed, physically done in.

'Welcome to the land of work, Spinx,' I thought to myself.

Tuesday morning arrived all too quickly. I dragged myself up and went through the motions. I was experiencing Groundhog Day as I met Susan and Pops at the bus stop. The day panned out pretty much the same as the previous one. I was stuck in the packaging room all day, along with Andrea; I packed a vast number of trays with floured baps, and my back pain was not getting any better. That night I got home looking worn out and very drained.

'You look knackered, son,' said my mother.
'I feel it. Don't know if I can go in tomorrow,' I replied.

'Well, don't' answered my mam.

I made the first executive decision of my life. I was not enjoying the work, and making £10 a day, four days a week, had to be easier than this. I went round to see Pops, to tell him I was wrapping in.

'What, after only two days?' he answered.

'It's bloody killing me, I replied. 'At this rate, I'm not going to be alive to spend the money!'

'Nee sweat,' said Pops. 'I'll tell the gaffer you can't work any more.'

The following night, he came round with my wages. After my pay was worked out, I finished up with £18 for the two days. I spent the money on a baseball shirt and a pair of Geordie jeans.

After I quit, Pops asked Bun Smith if he fancied a job at the bakery. He grabbed the opportunity with both hands and lasted in the job for nearly nine months, until the premature closure of the place. Bun worked every Sunday and most holidays. He showed me up in a way, for my pitiful attempt had lasted only two days. All I can say is, he must have been a tougher man than me!

I did work with Pops again. The following summer, he got jobs with a cleaning company for Neil and me, at Benton Hypermarket. We did four weeks' work and got paid absolutely nothing. The woman in charge took our bank details but we never saw any wages. Apparently, some of the staff were taking cash in hand and not declaring it to the taxman. The company was raided one night at the store and quite a few people looked sheepish as the DHSS inspector asked for names, dates of birth and National Insurance numbers. We were all finished that night and none of us saw a penny for our efforts. I mopped a lot of floors and dusted shelves but received nothing in return. However, I do have the lasting memory of Popeye lying flat on his back, cleaning a bottom shelf, while going warp speed down the aisle.

Good morning, Rothbury

NEIL: In April 1988, during the Easter holidays, nine young chaps from the streets of Costa del Cowgate and sunny Slatyford decided to test themselves with a three-night camping venture among the grassy knolls of Northumberland.

I can recall with delight that beautiful, bright morning, as we all merrily helped young Tootsie's old man, Dave, load up his van with our tents and supplies. These were to house and feed us throughout our exploration into the deep unknown.

The lucky nine were:
Paul "Tootsie" Grey
Justin "Vidal Sassoon" Crawford

Mickey "Rambo" Miller
Neil "Drago" Davis
Paul "Flappy" Durkin
Darren "Furry Lamb" Patterson
Scott "Nasal" Smith
Jason "Coco"/"Pops" Allison and
Scott "Scotty" Fenton

'Okay, lads, where to?' quipped Dave, as we all sat snugly in the back of his great big, off-white Ford Transit van, Mark 3, at the corner of Hayden Place, Slatyford, in Newcastle's delightful west end. 'Where should I head for on this most joyous of adventures?'

The nine of us exchanged confused shrugs and glances. In the excitement of organising the jaunt, we had somehow managed to overlook the small and delicate point of where we were actually going.

'Er, tell you what, Fatha, here's the deal. You drive and we'll tell you when we're there.'

'Ahey, that sounds about right. Yee drive, Dave, and we'll let you know when we've arrived,' agreed the others.

'Flipping imbeciles,' muttered Mr Grey under his breath, before slamming his foot to the floor, sending his load of children and tents crashing into one another.

'Urgh, the gypsy bas… ,' groaned Durkin from beneath four of his chums, as our ride rounded the corner on two wheels, heading north.

Two hours later and it seemed we had arrived. Well, sort of. Screeching to a halt, deep within Rothbury, Northumberland, Tootsie's dad turned out his merry cargo, with the gear and equipment, at the roadside at the top of a hill.

'Okay, guys, you are here. See you in three days. Have fun and hey, no bumming each other!'
With that, he roared off sharpish into the sunset.

'Oh well,' sniggered Bun and Popeye, jumping over a fence and heading down the steep bank. 'Looks like we're staying. Come on, lads, we'd better get wor tents up before it gets proper dark and that like.'

By early evening, (within the hour, in fact), four fine two-man tents stood proud and firm, shaded by trees, on the bank of the racing river.

'Hey, Jackie belter,' smiled Crawford as he admired the neat arrangement.

Eight seconds later...

''Ere, you cannot put yer f-f-f bleeding tents here,' screeched a rather disgruntled passing farmer/git.

Another hour later and 300 yards further on, we were once again ready and able to offer our sleeping bags a more than trustworthy place to rest their 95% polyester. With the fresh water lapping against the bank, we settled down outside the tents for a bite to eat, before the sun decided it was time to take the night off. As the band of brothers tucked into Bounty bars, Wagon Wheels and tuna and sweetcorn combos, young Durk sat there motionless, without a sandwich or Blue Riband in sight.

'Hey, where's yer bait [food]?' asked Mickey Miller, who was sporting a fetching black Rambo bandana around his napper.

'Oh, to hell with that,' shrugged Durk, with a grin. 'If I'm feeling the urge for some nosebag, I'll go catch it.'

'You'll bleeding what?' screamed Fenton and Crawford, spraying poor Furry Lamb with an array of Heinz ploughman and pickled onion crinkle-cut wedges.

'You heard me. If Stallone can do it in First-frigging-Blood, then so can I. That's right, lads, for these next three days, I'm living off the land.' The rest of us rolled around in hysterics as Durkin proceeded to wet his finger to test the wind, before heading across the grassy marsh and away into the trees, to claim his organic bounty.

'Hey, he's totally serious,' cried Popeye, looking in Spinx's rucksack.

'He's not brought any food.'

Some seventeen minutes later, our weary chum broke through the cover of the trees and headed our way. He had a couple of nasty-looking nettle stings and his rumbling tummy could be heard across the border.

'Hey, where's your wild boar and chips?' hollered Bun.

As the hysteria subsided slightly, Crawford and Miller cautiously quizzed the dinner-less one.

'Er, Spinx, what were you actually hoping to catch out there tonight?'

Feeling the tension ease, the rest of us managed to stop laughing for a moment as our hungry pal replied solemnly, 'To be honest, I've nee idea. I suppose something like a vole or, perhaps, a beaver.'

'A beaver!' The tears rolled down Crawford's cheeks.

'Listen, Paul,' smiled Miller, taking over. 'Just say you had caught something small, such as a rabbit, you're hardly the kind of guy to just kill it. If you had caught a sweet little bunny, you'd have been more likely to try romancing the bugger than eat it.'

Later, Durk tucked into a prawn-mayo special (one of Netto's finest), kindly supplied by Toots, who could not bear to see a demented mate go a second longer without his calcium and important daily minerals.

Finally, as the moon claimed the sunny sky, we decided on a much-needed game of Kill the Fox. By now, considering there was a lack of street lights plotted around our forest, it was deemed that the game would be played in the pitch dark. That night, one of the most successful games in Batter the Fox history was carried out. For on that occasion we had it all.

Firstly, we had the space on which to roam and this itself brought a host of unprecedented and endless possibilities to our insane, merry band of soldiers of fortune.

Secondly, and more importantly, we had two good teams, more than willing to kick the living hell out of each other.

We fixed our warpaint and the game commenced. My four-man unit, Fenton, Pops, Bun and I, was first to flee. We made it like the wind to the top of the hill and the cover of the trees.

Down in the valley, at base camp, the others waited. With his trusted Casio, Durkin counted away the five minutes that my team had to leg it. Crawford and Furry checked their torches.

Meanwhile, in a dense thicket, Pops glanced, without a word, up through the treetops. His trademark smirk was visible even in the shadows and the rest of us soon realised he was up to something.

Some fifty feet below, the five-man Team Alpha began to separate and move widely, spreading their torch light far into the night.

'Listen,' whispered Popeye, 'I've an idea. Let's get ourselves up into these trees, as high as we can. Come on, they've started.'

He shimmied his way up a 30-foot pine lady-of-the-forest.

As Team Alpha raced in our direction with their sticks, Fenton and Bun both slipped silently aloft and out of sight. Popeye's simple plan was proving flawless. I urge you to acknowledge my sheer amazement at what happened next.

Just as I wrapped my arms and legs around the nearest tree, the whole thing gave way with an almighty crunching snap and a whoosh. It sent me roaring with intense speed down the hillside, in total darkness, still firmly clutching the dead and hollow birch.

'Aaaaeeeh!' I screamed into the night, as I raced like a steam train over the muddy grass with my new leafy friend.

'What the hell was that?' enquired Miller and Toots, from their vantage point, midway up the hillside, as I ploughed on nervously.

Eventually, I came to a stop, thirty feet shy of the river. Finding my feet, I focused long and hard into the distance, calculating my next move. Suddenly, I was felled from behind with a knee-height drop kick and was promptly placed under arrest with some swish and tasty handiwork from Toots and Mickey Miller. Next, I found both of my hands behind my back, bound tight with a pair of Furry Lamb's socks.

'Crawford, we've caught one!' they shouted as they led me back to their lock-up (the tents) for my de-briefing.

Ten seconds later, led by Commander Crawford, the others returned to base camp, smirking.

'Okay, Davis,' sighed Crawford, rubbing his Ninja stick, 'where are they?' Checking my escape routes, I coughed nervously and shrugged.

'How the hell would I know? I just fell 200 feet down that frigging hillside!'

As the others howled with laughter, Mr C continued.

'Was that you? Hell's teeth, Davis, I thought there had been a landslide.'

'That makes two of us,' I retorted, hoping to shift attention away from my tree-bound chums.

Unfortunately for yours truly, this did not work.

'Give them up, or it's an ass-whopping,' sniggered Crawford.

Foolishly, I shrugged , 'Who?'

'Okay, lads,' nodded Mr C, heading back into the darkness. 'Bust him up royally!'

Thirty-five minutes and one severe ass-whopping later, I lay tied up on the grass outside our row of flapping tents. Young Toots was on guard, sitting on a deck chair while the others of his team were still out, searching far and wide for my brave troop. As I lay there, chatting away with Toots, Popeye came racing from nowhere, with a piercing "Hii-yaa!" He took poor Toots from behind with an incredible low-flying close line, knocking the unfortunate fellow right out of his comfy deck chair and onto the ground.

'Frigging hell, Popeye,' I hailed from the deck, next to my four-eyed foe, who was now out cold. 'I think you killed the specky swine.'

'Nee time for that right now,' chirped my kung-fu friend as he untied my hands. 'Come on, we'd better get this little stroker tied up before he comes to.'

Fenton and Bun appeared from behind the bushes.

'Frigg me, Pops,' they gasped. 'What have you done to him?'

'Never mind that,' barked Popeye, as he finished binding Tootsie's arms to the back of the upturned deck chair. 'Fenton, hurry up and tie his feet to something. It looks like he's waking up.'

And then, as our dear young semi-comatose pal voiced the words:

'What in the flying...... just happ.....?' Team Alpha pounced like a panther. Finding my feet once more, I fled out of there, towards the river.

Unbeknown to me, Durkin and Furry were fast on my trail. With a spinning Boom! the three of us found ourselves heading downstream in a hurry, trading blows under the icy, watery current.

Meanwhile, back on dry land, it was a full-blown free-for-all. Scotty Fenton put the poor, hapless Tootsie back in the land of Nod with a splendid bear-hug tactic. And Popeye, who had somehow managed to wrap his sleeping bag round the head of the dumbfounded Mickey M, was going great guns until Master Crawford took him out with a trademark right-hander.

Fifteen minutes of mayhem later, we were all back by the tents, sharing a hand and a laugh. However, Furry, Durk and I had been swept almost two miles downstream and had a rather chilly walk home to the warmth of our waiting tents and sleeping bags. Then, as our gang of loving chums bid bonne nuit to the sweet night, the rains came

Folks, when I say rain, I mean rain. It came down like a monsoon for the next twelve hours. By the time daylight finally showed its sarcastic face, our tents had more water in them than the fish at Niagara Falls.

'Jesus H Christ!' came the call from Justin's tent, which he shared with the Lamb and Miller. 'You could paddle a frigging canoe in this son-of-a-bitch.'

Meanwhile, my tent buddy, Scotty Fenton, (who in some four years' time would be my cabin mate on the good old QE2), slept on, oblivious to the fact that pretty soon, we would be needing our armbands.

'Scott, wake the hell up! We're taking some serious water in this nylon abode.'

Jumping to his feet, he began to panic at the sight of the twelve-inch wall of water rolling from our tent zip and heading his way.

'Davis, what have you done?'

Two tents away, Durkin and Tootsie were soon awake, and aware of the mini-Armageddon which was unfolding.

'What the flying… ?' screamed Durk as he fell out of the tent in his sodden boxer shorts, letting out a breaking wave of water at the same time.

'What the hell happened?'

Around him, young chaps ran amok, with dripping asses in their wet sleeping attire. Popeye and Bun had already done a runner; they had caught the bus first thing in the morning.

'Bloody hell, lads,' said Toots, 'should I call me fatha?'

'Na, listen,' voiced the man of reason, Master Fenton. 'The rains have passed us by now and, if I'm not mistaken, those skies out there are blue. Come on, let's hang everything on the trees to dry, and have a little breakfast.'

'Bugger me, Scott, nee wonder you are second in command in the Scouts,' sighed Durk and I, humbly.

A vote was taken and the remaining seven of us decided to stay. One and all approved and welcomed a brisk walk into town for some much-needed supplies. With the wind in our hair, we set off to shop for things such as adult magazines and, hopefully, to get the opportunity to point at and heckle the strange-looking village people whom we expected to encounter in downtown Rothbury.

It was a fine mid-afternoon jaunt and we marched together at an impressive speed, hands behind our backs, from the river into the town, which was a good two miles away.

I daresay that, from up high, we young boys from the brook must have resembled a pack of demented stallions as we roared along on our village-bound quest. We later named this ridiculous walk as the Wacky Races. Here is an idiot's guide to perfecting the Wacky Races stance:

No.1 Firstly, acquire at least six or seven of your closest friends, school chums or colleagues and form into a straight line formation.

No.2 Now, with your unit of fine gents or finer ladies facing the chosen angle of projection, eg village or dirt path, slide leading foot forward, sucking in stomach at the same time, ready for impending action.

No.3 Finally, ease whole of body's weight onto leading leg, while pointing out chin to full extent, and draw into perfect line with other contestants.

On the order Hike! stride forward as fast as humanly possible, with hands tightly together and chin upright at all times. Continue your sprint with all your energy and might, without switching your stance for a second, even if this means heading straight for a road, ditch or stationary vehicle. Good luck and happy tidings! May you give the Wacky Races your true, undivided devotion until your dying day. If you do it properly, it may not be that long!

Later, in the town, we somehow managed to be escorted from two public houses and two newsagents. Our first offence was due to our being some four years shy of the legal tasting age. The second was our accidentally knocking down the entire top shelf within some outlet, in our desperate pursuit of the April edition of Big-Jugs-R-Us.

As we headed back to the comfort and sanctuary of the tents, we passed a local guy of some 65-plus years who was a dead cert for the missing love-child of Postman Pat.

Two days later, our adventure was over. Tootsie's old man had driven only about twenty miles towards home before we all realised we had forgotten the tents!

'Morning, Rothbury. In our hearts you shall remain forever.

Chapter 12

The things we do for love...

Mel...

I recall it was slap bang in the middle of the baking summer of 85 that our band of merry men first ever clapped eyes on the delightful Mel, the younger sister of our new pal Wayne from Halifax, West Yorkshire. It's very accurate to suggest that our morning game of world cup doubles outside the Blue door ended the second she took a seat opposite on the curb. Blue eyes and wonderful blonde curly hair, it's safe to say we in total were well and truly hooked!

'I'm def marring her!' Quacked Bun.

'As if? I saw her first retorted Pops in an instant. Ensuing a 15 minute debate between them both, almost ending in a fist fight!?

Looking back, it was obvious from the outset that Melanie was nothing like the other girls whom graced our estate? Perhaps it was her friendly familiar smile, not to mention her very deep foxy Yorkshire accent which had reduced the 8 of us into nervous wrecks. One thing however was certain as we all sped home that day, desperate to find our fill of both toothpaste and shower gel...we were all together at once...in love!!!

Whatever her power was, this very same mutual effect had the 8 of us back that very next day, armed with our very best attire and stinking soundly to the high hills of Brute!

A peculiar sight, we must have drawn, as we stood there that summer morning, shuffling our feet while sporting our Sunday best and doing everything to avoid kicking the ball.

I can recall fondly, how dashing young Popeye looked that day, kitted out in his Farah slacks and black matching tank-top a young Errol Flynn in the making. Unlike Mr Henton, who for some reason had opted to attend the day's courtship, dressed in full tennis mode! He'd even brought along a matching head band and racket! A peculiar event in itself when you consider there wasn't a court to play on for at least five miles in any direction?

And with young Melanie again watching from the curb side, the next course of actions would define the last two weeks of the summer of 85...A free for all!

Squinting with the sun in her eyes, Mel without realising it, had unintentionally given Bun the green light with what appeared to be a smile? Sensing his luck was indeed in, our nasal having chum proceeded to mince over towards her by the curb. Hearing only wedding bells, our dear brother failed to notice Popeye's screaming left hook connect with his chin? Leaving him crudely KO'd on the spot!

Later still and long after Davy Henton had ran both Durkin and Ingram into a near-by fence chin first, in what can only be described as a double head breaker?
Our entire merry gang had vowed never to speak or seek solace from one another again!

Two days later however, a vote was conducted and with a winning majority vote of 5-3 Durkin Jnr I'm happy to report was given the green light to go steady with wor Mel.

He'd just have to run it by her first?

For Mel...the one who stole our summer hearts and opened our eyes to the benefits with bathing more than twice a month.

PAUL: For the first time, as a group of friends, we started to notice the opposite sex a tad more. I'm not kidding myself, Wayne's good looks and charisma were always head and shoulders above the rest of ours (as was his quiff!), but this made it easier for us to approach girls and strike up a conversation.

In the midst of all this, Wayne had a younger sister, Melanie, who was very beautiful. She had blonde, curly hair, piercing blue eyes and an hourglass figure. It would be a lie to say most of the chaps didn't want to rub lips with her, but like most things, she was out of our league. Also, Wayne would have pulled our heads off if we had tried to snog his younger sis. I thought I had more chance of getting crap from a rocking horse than of actually "seeing" Melanie, so I admired from afar and kept my head down.

The other lads were not backward in coming forward when it came to women.

'Any chance of a tongue sarnie?' was one of Popeye's opening lines. Suffice to say, it never really worked.

I was a lot shyer than the rest of the chaps, so I tended to take a back seat when they were using their patter on girls. Probably for this reason, they all thought I was a faggot or a homo. I didn't have a proper girlfriend until I was seventeen, so I can now see why they thought I was gay.

Going back to Melanie, though, I found out from Wayne that she had a soft spot for me.

'Our Melanie likes ya, Flappy,' he said, one summer evening. 'She said you are really sweet and she thinks ya dead good-looking.'

'Really? Does she wear glasses?' I replied.

Back then, I had (and still have) very little confidence in myself. This may be one of the reasons I was not forthcoming with the opposite sex. It was hard to get my head around the fact that Melanie liked me. I tried to think of reasons why she was attracted to me, but came up with none.

'Wow,' I gasped. 'I'm really flattered but she is far too good for me.'

'Well, dude, I think she's going to ask you out. What would you say?' asked Wayne.

My heart started racing and I got all nervous. I did not know how to answer Wayne's question. I had never had a girlfriend and starting a relationship with Melanie would throw up all sorts of problems. Where would I take her? Would we hold hands? What would the other lads say? And most importantly, would I have to kiss her? French kissing was something I had practised on the back of my hand, but never with a female. I was worried that I was going to swallow her whole if my technique was not correct. My heart was shouting, "Yes, yes, go out with her, you fool," but my head was saying, "Don't bother; you'll just make an idiot of yourself." I was confused but tried to make a joke of it.

'Stop winding me up, Wayne,' I said.

'I'm not, man. She really does like you. Anyway, you won't have long with her; we're away home on Friday.'

Wayne and Melanie only spent the holidays in Newcastle. They would soon be heading back to their father's house in Halifax. It was nearing the end of the six-week summer break and they were due back in West Yorkshire in a couple of days. This gave me a little breathing space and the opportunity I needed. I could say yes to Melanie and kill two birds with one stone. The boys would be as jealous as f*ck and they would no longer think I was afraid of girls.

'Stuff it, of course I will go out with her,' I said.

'No bother,' replied Wayne. 'I'll go and tell her now.'

With that, he dropped the ball he had been kicking against the wooden fence of the Tavern playing field, and headed across the street to his home. My heart raced faster with the realisation of what had just happened. I had been asked out before by a few girls; Angie Laws, Pamela Kipling and Michelle Davis spring to mind. However, I had bottled out of going out with any of them. Now, Melanie Aldred, the girl whom all the chaps wanted, was going to be my girlfriend. Wayne disappeared inside the house for a few moments then came back, holding one thumb aloft.

'Sorted, mate. You are now officially a couple,' he said.

I felt the colour drain from my face. I turned to see Melanie standing at her front door, waving to me. Nervously, I waved back and gave a half-hearted smile.

'What have I done,' I thought.

At this time, Popeye, Neil and John had made their way into the street. Wayne passed the ball down to Popeye who, in true style, blasted the thing full belt, straight over the Tavern fence.

'Tell them the news, Flappy,' Wayne said.

'What news?' I replied, acting dumb.

'You know what. Here, lads, Paul is seeing our Mel.'

'You spawny git!' snapped Pops.

'It must be for a bet,' piped in John.

'Can I have a gan when you're finished, Spinx?' said Neil.

'Get stuffed, the lot of you,' I hit back.

The boys shook their heads and proceeded on to the Tavern for a game of World Cup singles. I don't think they believed it and, to be fair, neither did I. During the game, they made some snidey but funny references to Melanie and me, but I just laughed them off.

The following day, I found out that Wayne and Melanie were leaving and probably would not be back until Christmas, or maybe the following Easter. We all spent our last night together, hanging around the Blue door, playing football and listening to LL Cool J on Wayne's Matsui ghetto blaster. I had talked briefly to Melanie that night, but tried to act cool in front of the other lads, to convey that it was no big deal, going out with this gorgeous 15-year-old girl.

As the evening drew to a close, the lads started to make their way home and I hung about for a while. Wayne headed for his house and I waved as he went in.

'See you soon, pal,' I said.

'Yeah, mate. Keep this lot in order and I'll catch up with you shortly,' replied Wayne.

For the past two years, I had built myself up for this moment and it was finally going to happen. I was going to swap saliva with a person of the opposite sex. Mel and I stood on the steps leading to the house and waited for Wayne to close the door. My heart was racing: this was it! Mel took my hand and looked into my eyes.

'Goodnight, Paul. Hope to see you soon.'

I puckered up and closed my eyes, then…. Nothing. I opened up to see the front door being shut in my face. What a let down.

Thinking about it, Melanie was probably as nervous as I was. Or, perhaps, she realised that, close up, I looked like a bulldog licking urine off a nettle. Anyhow, the fact of the matter is, I stood there like a lemon for a few minutes, wondering what the hell had just happened. I trundled off home, partly relieved, partly sad about the whole thing. As expected, the boys wanted all the details.

'Did you do it?'

'Divv'nt be daft. I just got a kiss.'

'So you're not gay after all!'

'Never was. Just waiting for the right lass.'

'Well, you'll have a long wait, cos she's not coming back until next Easter,' said John.

'She's worth waiting for, man. She's a fine looking lady,' chipped in Pops.

He was right: she was definitely worth waiting for. In fact, I'm still bloody waiting some nineteen years on. I had told a small lie, as I never actually kissed Melanie. I said that I had, so that the lads would not take the micky out of me. When Melanie returned to Newcastle the following spring, she had a new boyfriend in Halifax. I was a distant memory. Wayne broke the news to me and, in truth, I wasn't that bothered. It had been more of a status thing. Going out with Melanie Aldred kept me in good stead with the boys. It also gave me an excuse if another girl came sniffing; I could say I was seeing someone. Everyone was a winner! With that, I don't know if you can count Melanie as my first proper girlfriend. Going out with her for one and a half days without even a kiss, may be stretching it a bit.

Coming off the back of that 'love story' leads me nicely into a memory that still makes me laugh out loud. Naturally, we were all virgins at this time and we wondered who would be first to pop his cherry. Girls were not really in the equation until Wayne came along. We found, though, the older we got, the more pressured we felt regarding sex.

I suppose every teenager (male and female) goes through the same thing in regards of losing their virginity. Apart from one of the chaps, I believe none of us had 'done the deed' but it was about to present itself one summer evening. To keep the identity of the two Romeos secret, I'll just call them Mr X and Mr Y! Unfortunately, I was spending the night at Lee and Lloyd's house in Gosforth, so never got to witness any of the events that night, but I'm correctly informed the below account is what happened.

It was an average summer night at around 7 o'clock. The lads were doing their normal things on the Tavern. Following a game of football, they decided to climb trees to pass the time. In the distance, a figure appeared, approaching the boys. As it got closer, it dawned on them who it was.

'Oh great. here comes that Plumley lass' said Henton, as Miss Vicky Plumley came into sight.

'What does she want now?' asked Johnny Ingram.
Vicky Plumley was a local girl from around the area. Although we didn't know her very well, her name and face were well known throughout Cowgate. There had been a few rumours that she liked the guys, if you get my meaning!

'What you up to?' shouted Plumley at us.

'Nothing much' barked back Popeye 'Just messing around up here'. The lads continued along the treeline until we met the first corner.

'I'm bored now' said Henton, and proceeded to climb off the tree. The rest of the lads followed, all dismounting from the trees.

'Who fancies a game of football?' said Neil

'Yeah, why not' replied Micky F.

'Okay, we'll head across to the blue door' said Neil.

At this point they started walking across the field towards the dairy, to have a game of soccer. Now, this is when events started to unfold. 'Mr X' started to drop back with Miss Plumley and seemed to get into a deep conversation with her. The rest of the chaps headed for the gates, when a panting Mr X, ran up and approached them. The gist of his story, when he managed to get his breath back, was Miss Plumley was feeling a bit frisky and had offered a couple of the boys their step from being a boy into manhood!

Apparently the lads looked a bit shocked but a couple appeared to be mulling it over.

'Where will this take place?' asked one of the lads.

'Corner of the field' replied Mr X.

'Any protection on offer?' asked another.

'Yeah' replied X 'she's come prepared!'

After a few minutes discussion, five of the boys decided against it. Maybe they were saving themselves for someone special or maybe a bit nervous about the whole losing their virginity issue. That left Mr X and Mr Y, who had decided that tonight was going to be the night. After a long discussion, Mr Y headed over to the corner of the Tavern playing field, where Miss Plumley was waiting. He returned several minutes later to the blue door, looking rather pleased with himself.

'Well?' asked one of the chaps.

'That was mint' replied Mr Y.

Judging it was his first sexual experience, in hindsight, I'm not sure it was 'mint' (slang word for great).

I don't believe any of the other lads asked for more details than that, as if they had've been interested, I suppose they would have found out for themselves if Miss Plumley was 'mint'!

Mr X then headed off across the field. He came back around fifteen minutes later.

'Well, was it mint?' asked one of the lads.

'I think she loved every minute of it' answered Mr X.

The lads laughed out loud at Mr X's remark but believed it was the truth! Twenty minutes after the proposal, all the lads were playing football, as if nothing had happened. Miss Plumley passed a few minutes later, gave a smile to Mr X and Y, and disappeared up the street. Every boy goes through the transition and on that August summer evening, two of the Blue Door gang made the leap into adulthood. Without pointing any fingers however, I can confirm that neither Mr Henton, Mr Davis nor Mr Ingram were indeed either Mr Y or Mr X!

NEIL: I was nine years old when my parents' marriage went off the tracks. It took a long time for me to get used to the fact that my father was not going to be around

that much any more. As with any other kid, it made me a little mad. For the first few years, I suppose, again like any other kid, I was convinced that one day, he would just come back. He didn't, of course, and to be fair, he and my mother were better off apart. Back then, domestic wars were common and bitter-fought. Any good soul knows that wars are no good for children and, it seemed, this break-up would at last bring some calm.

Weekends were different. In the beginning, my big sis and I would have the time of our lives, with our crazy old pop leading the way. No matter where we ended up – Spanish City, down at Whitley Bay, or at the West Jesmond cinema, watching Rocky Balboa through 1 to 3 – we always had fun. One thing which would never stop hurting, however, was that look of sadness in my dear dad's eyes, as he turned to wave goodbye for yet another long week. Yeah, looking back, I never got over that one.

Another thing which pained me was the thought of his being alone. At that time, I did not have my merry band of Chutney boys around me, to chase away the tears. Full stop, I needed the guy who just two years ago had climbed his ladder on Christmas Eve, to ring bells outside our bedroom window so that we would know that Santa Claus was back in town. Yeah, I needed that guy all right.

In future years, our relationship would certainly suffer, but in the end we have managed to claw back all those years.

Now I am the one with a child and I know that one day it will be my turn to explain why daddy is not there with mummy any more. Truth is, my lad, I guess we all make mistakes, no matter how hard we try to avoid them. Though you, my Son, were definitely never one of them.

'No, my boy,' I will say. 'You were the one thing in both our lives which really did make some kind of sense... x'

Today, in our role as parents, we constantly ask one another whether we could do more: more for that child, more for our children. Who knows the answer? Not you or I. However, I did remember not so long ago that all I really needed as a kid, apart from love, was time. Ask any kid out there today and he will probably tell you the very same thing. Forget race. Forget gender. No amount of money will save the deal either. In my experience, time – a parent's time - was what really made the difference. (And obviously, toys worked too!!) Another way of looking at it is this. The more a child feels loved and wanted by his or her folks, the less that child will be willing to hurt them in the future.

Ha yeah, that's how I used to see it. Just a little piece of truth in there, folks.

Sometimes, holed up in this job, time is all we have. A week away from the people you love most can feel like years. You step on board prepared, alert and ready for work, yet the best part of you wishes you were back at home, playing with your kids. For my eleven year old, I know, it is not easy. It is simple enough, he just wants his dad and his dad just wants him too. But this is the job and that's what we take to pay the bills. So do a lot of other folk; we certainly are not alone.

Chapter 13

The red hut

As the Blue Door gang got older and interest in girls intensified, we started looking for new ways to meet the fine young ladies of Cowgate and Blakelaw. One meeting place was the Red Hut, on the outskirts of Blakelaw. This was an old, run-down pre-fabricated building that was the focal point of the community and the surrounding areas. Events were held there on a daily basis, ranging from bingo to line-dancing. Every Monday and Thursday evening, it was the turn of the local youths to get down and dirty to the newest and funkiest music in the top forty. Up to the age of fourteen or fifteen, we were not that bothered about hanging out at such venues, but the Hut became the "in" place so we decided to give it a bash.

The closest we had been to a Hut event was playing five-a-side football on the outdoor courts that lay adjacent to the place. On a few occasions, when playing football, we had seen teenagers of about our age, dressed in their smartest Farah dress trousers and pink Le Shark polo shirts, walking with a swagger into the Red Hut. Although curious, we carried on with our game and ignored the loud music and laughter coming from the disco next to us. It was not our scene at the time, but we succumbed to all the hype and became regulars.

After paying the 20p entrance fee, you would make your way into the main room. The Hut was a bit like Dr Who's Tardis. It looked quite small from outside, but in fact, it was very spacious. The curtains were drawn to stop the sunlight entering on summer evenings. Chairs lined the two longest walls, parallel to each other. At the top end lay the DJ stand, with two large speakers either side of the turntables. I recognised the kid who used to "spin the decks" as a former sixth form student from Blakelaw School. At the other end of the Hut were the toilets, next to the tuck shop. The aroma of home-made toffee cakes wafted through into the main room from time to time.

Entering the disco, we would usually head straight for the tuck shop, for we always seemed to be hungry. A packet of Tudor crisps and a toffee cake later, we were ready to rock. We would also purchase a bottle of Panda Cola to take over to where we were standing. Thirsty work, this dancing lark! As with most discos, people had their favourite music, therefore a steady stream of dancers came and went from the floor. Madonna was always a good artiste to get people up to dance and most kids would lose their minds when the DJ played "Never Gonna Give You Up" by Rick Astley.

My lasting memory is of the night when Popeye was dancing to Kim Wilde's "Keep Me Hanging On". Although no John Travolta, Pops had some good moves on him. He had this kind-of shimmy/slide that made Michael Jackson's Moonwalk look like a piece of cake. Imagine Pops with both arms in the air, swaying from side to side. Then, with one foot on the floor at all times, the other foot would come behind it, making a kind of X shape with his legs. Other kids were mesmerised by this dance and many tried to copy it… but failed. This night, Pops had shimmied from one end of the Hut to the other. The DJ decided to use the smoke machine to create a little more atmosphere, forgot to turn it off after its thirty-second cycle and thus pumped enough smoke into the place to make everything black out. Among the coughing and sputtering crowd, a gap appeared and Pops came hurtling through like a bull in a china shop. Halfway into his sprint, he did a small jump and landed on his knees, skidding the rest of the way down the hall. He passed us with the speed of a Formula 1 racing car and disappeared into the engulfing smoke.

A cry of, 'Oh, ya bugger!' came from the smoke into which Pops had vanished. He had managed to slide head first into the DJ stand, knocking over the turntables. Ms Wilde had just gone into her second verse but screeched to an almighty halt.

'Pops, Pops,' I shouted, 'are you okay?'

'Aye,' replied a voice through the smoke, 'but I think the DJ is gooshed.'

The ladies serving in the tuck shop came running out to see what all the commotion was. When the smoke cleared, all they could see was a pair of Adidas "Kick" protruding from behind the DJ stand. Everyone crowded round the stand and peered over. Pops was dusting himself off after another uncanny mishap. Groans and moans came from our now semi-conscious DJ friend. Popeye did the decent thing and tried to help him to his feet. The DJ's JVC headphones were wrapped around his neck and his fake Ray-Ban sunglasses now lay crooked on his nose.

'You haven't got "Diamond Lights" by Glenn and Chris, have you, mate?' asked Pops, while steadying the guy.

'You just broke my Technics turntables and you're asking if I can play a song by a pair of flippin' footballers!' replied the DJ.

'Aye, it's a cracking tune. Not only is Waddle a wizard on the wing, but he's got a cracking pair of lungs,' said Pops.

'I'm ganna bloody kill you!' screamed the now livid turntable maestro.

As he lunged, his headphone wire caught on his vast record collection and pulled him backwards.

'I take it ya divvn't dee requests, then,' chirped Pops.

'Think it's time to leave,' I suggested.

We all made a bolt for the door and kept on running.

'How was I to know he was gannna fill the room with smoke,' he said to us.

He had a valid point. We lay low for a couple of weeks and eventually Popeye apologised to the DJ for his little accident.

The Popeye shuffle was in full swing for some time at the Red

Hut, but Pops was a tad more cautious when adding the slide into the equation.

The Hut is now gone. It was pulled down about five years ago; only derelict and bushes remain. I passed recently while visiting my mother and had a little chuckle to myself. At least I can say I saw the master in his prime.

NUFC

How fast these months seem to pass. By now, of course, October 2011 and as the crow flies, we stand unbeaten and 3rd place in the table? An un-believable achievement, for a club, whom just sacrificed it's three best players. With local Boy Andy Carroll £35m to Liverpool, Joey (light's out Barton QPR (Free) and finally Kevin Nolan (West ham) £5m! A lot of Cash came in and at present hardly a penny has been spent on any new recruits? Making our shock standing in the Premier league all the more surprising!

As per usual, just when things seem to be going swimmingly, a spanner as always is thrown into the works? And as more usual than often, It usually involves our Play-boy come Cockney-wide boy Owner...One Michael Ashley. No stranger to trouble and pre-meditated wind-ups, young Mike, has tried and succeeded to both alienate and provoke every single NUFC fan and critic on the globe!

I'm sure, like any football fan, or regional die-hard, you too have read all the negativity that seems to both follow and engulf our great Club, kicking off any wheels of momentum that have grown, as they go? Now Mike, has pulled out another master stroke and perhaps his most damaging one to date!

Yes after 118 years of the fans Theatre, which is has always been known as St James Park...Will now be addressed as, wait for it...'The Sports Direct Arena' Very catchy if your, either deaf, dumb and on the verge of following Ice hockey from now on!

Just another fans view, on all things black and white.

I really have no idea how our group of young street trash became so industrious and imaginative in the face of all the depression and uncertainty which seemed to have gripped Tyneside by the throat. I suppose our only incentive was to look out for one another. We were never about stealing other people's possessions. No, for us it was all about adventure and a voyage into the unknown.

Growing up and finding work were never mentioned or on our agenda. For one thing, there was no work to go to, not in Newcastle in 1985. We grew up with Auf Wiedersehn Pet flashing on our TV sets every Sunday night. Even at such a young age, we knew only too well what poor Neville and Dennis were going through, out there in their smelly German hut. We had seen that same desperate look in the eyes of our own parents. For us, outgrowing our faded Geordie jeans and getting old was just not going to happen.

At the age of twelve, you really do believe that you and the pals you dote on will always stay as they are. In many ways, this was my one pure reason and it influenced my decision to write this tale about our childhood. The pledge that we made as kids, to always stays young, has not been broken. Okay, I am not going to exaggerate and say we have never changed, or that we still hang around and go everywhere together as we used to. Our lives and circumstances have scattered us far but the friendships endure.

In the last sixteen years, I have sailed from one port to another on ships, chasing the change at the bottom of the ocean. Somehow I ended up as a deck-hand in the Merchant Navy. How this actually occurred, I'll never know.

Naturally, the others too have fled the Cowgate nest, but I still find it incredible that none of us has really changed. There is no uncomfortable silence when we run into one another. I recall my thirtieth birthday, when we all met up for a night out on the beverage. Good old Flappy had sent out the e-mails. It was the first time in a long time that everyone managed to turn up, including some other special people, Lee

"Elvis" Jobling and his chick, Dawn. Even Wayne "I think she fancies me" Aldred made it from sunny Halifax. We had a cracking night. I remember standing there, my bottle of sweet Cornea (with lime slice) in hand, watching them all, with a smile on my face, as they laughed and caught up with each other's news.

It was so evident that nothing had changed between us. There was Pops, swinging Bun around like a rag doll, in his familiar bear-hug. By the bar, Micky F stood giggling like a schoolgirl with Davie H and John "Chuck Berry" Ingram. I bet that when we are chasing our pensions and dodging those coffins, we shall still be part of the very same scenes. Well, I pray that we shall.

Two Cowgate Jingles

Cowgate
Cowgate, she's in a state.
Her broken lines just won't go straight.
With the streets not cleaned, the rats grew fatter.
A thousand dreams, they wilt, they scatter.
It's not too late,
The light's still here; you just have to wait.
Cowgate, she's in a state.

Deep, so very deep!

Blue Door

Cobbled stones, they greet your path.
Part-time goals, you made us laugh.
Fun and games and a whole lot more,
Every night at the big Blue Door.
When you're lost, you'll find us there,
Little boys without a care.

Deeper still… I need a hug.

Chapter 14

Cowgate of present

NEIL: Not long ago, in March 2007, I called young Durkin at his busy office within the bustling complex of Newcastle University, for our daily chat. At once, he groaned,

'She's gone, bud.'

'Who has?' I asked, beginning to fret.

'The Blue Door, mate. They knocked her down yesterday. She's gone for good.'

Even though we had for some time been aware of the council's plans to rip down the Blue Door and the surrounding dairy area, when the day finally came, both of us felt crushed.

'Don't know what to say, mate,' I replied, feeling drained.

'Nor me, mucker,' rasped Durk. 'It feels so weird. We'll never see the old girl again.'

'Tell me about it,' I retorted. 'What's gonna happen to the Chinese now is beyond me!'

'Chinese?'

'Ahey, ye know the folks from China and that who will come over for the tour.'

'You've totally lost me here, kid.'

'Yee know, when the book goes global and the council have to start ferrying them in to se the sights.'

Oh, haaa, you crazy swine. Yes, now I see where you're coming from, Master Davis!' chuckled my mate, grasping my angle and lightening the mood.

However, in my mind I was deadly serious. Hey, why not? I couldn't give a monkey's toss if you are wetting yourself out there, laughing at my silly old dream. To me, it doesn't matter. Who else, I ask you, would dare to attempt putting our dear Cowgate back on the map? The fact that she was never on it fails to dampen my coals.

'So, what we gonna show them on this tour of ours?' I continued. My number one side-kick suggested, 'Er, we could always head past the place where Mr X and Mr Y lost their cherries with young Miss Plumley.'

'Sounds like a winner to me, my son!'

And so it was set. The tour of sunny Cowgate and all her glories was born. Ha, well, maybe…

Back in the summer of 2002 I myself went on one real such tour and pilgrimage. For many years I had dreamed of heading State-side, towards Boston and the tiny fishing town of Gloucester, Massachusetts, the home of the Perfect storm. Back in 1991, when the east coast of the United States was hit by the worst storm in living memory, I too was out at sea. Luckily, my ship was not in the same region, though eleven days earlier she had been. The thing about this so-called Perfect storm which gripped my imagination so strongly at the time, was the sheer, unrelenting force behind it. I have no idea why, but I have always been fascinated by the power of the sea. Ever since childhood, I had wondered just how bad it could get; you know, at its very worst.

So, the prospect of heading out to the place and to the people who had seen the storm firsthand was an absolute must for me. Having read Christian Jungler's book approximately ten times, I felt I was more than ready to explore this distant shore and float around there unnoticed for a little while, to take it all in. I am so glad that I made the trip.

I recall sipping a cold, sweet Budweiser one night in the formidable Crow's Nest (see the movie!) and thinking how close I felt to actually being inside the pages of Mr Jungler's book. It was surreal, for there, seated in exactly the same position at the end of the bar, was the very guy I'd seen in a photograph in the paperback. And there by the dartboard was list of approaching birthdays, among which was the name of the sister of one of the men who had gone down with the boat, Andrea Gail.

I do not think I have felt more humbled , or grateful to have been in a place, ever since.

Back to our Blue Door tour…

I can picture our tally of star-struck fine ladies and gents from near and far, heading over here to sunny Cowgate, to see for themselves some of the historic sites they read about and loved in the book.

I guess it would go something like this: 'Okay, folks, welcome here to the pristine surrounds of our sunny Cowgate. Over here, you will notice the brand new Aldi food store and less, former home of the sacred Ponteland Road dairy and the Blue Door itself. Yes, folks, this huge rear access shutter door was in the past used for such things as, er, a door, and also a part-time goal post by your little heroes in the book.'

Good up to now, eh?

'And now, folks, it's brace yourself time. For here we are in the shadow of the trees upon the fine turf of the Tavern playing fields. This, ladies and gents, is where our young scamps used to spend many an hour, swinging through the very same branches that are now above your heads. And yes, folks,' the cute, short-skirted female tour guide would quack, 'right now is camera time. For here by your feet is the very spot where two of the chaps took the step from being boys into men with a certain Miss Plumley.'

Those frigging tickets would sell like hot cakes. Hell's teeth, Cowgate would have to stick up at least half a dozen hotels to cater for the impending stampede. Who knows? Hey, if you are out there reading this, it must mean you bought the book, which also means that somehow we got the thing published. So already, we are almost halfway there.

Our Cowgate/Blue Door tour is almost a reality. Be sure to bring your camera, for who knows what we might find? I have it on good authority that our sweet Smyths still reside within the same four walls.

Also, it goes without saying that old Master Azlam and his sons , if you could find them, would be only too happy to pose for snapshots.

How about a mini detour to some of our own favourite six-foot privets and hedges? I and the rest of the Blue Door cast would be happy to dive over them for the modest sum of around £12 per demonstration. Okay, folks, I hear you. In short, we'd clear up!

You good people out there could easily, one day, be putting our sweet kids through college. It's that simple. Would you fly, say, eight thousand miles to stand over the historic site where one 12–year-old Popeye sampled the fruits of adulthood? If the answer is yes, then feel free to spread the word and let's get the guided tour (audio-cassette optional) off the ground and running.

Any one of you guys out there could easily put your foot down and advise your pretty, sincere wife or husband to forget trips to those everyday sights such as the Taj Mahal or China's Great Wall. Say, 'No, today we head for the tranquil setting and delights of the magical Blue Door, (now Netto's, mind), and we shall witness with pride and harmonic joy such venues as where the likes of one young John Ingram attempted to launch a golf ball through the window of that casual deli-mart, former abode of Master Azlam Muttel.'

I'll pull the rug over this topic with one final message and rant. Forget New York and frown upon the Golden Gate, for when you want to explore the time of your lives, head for the Tavern and Stamfi fields.

Cowgate – you'll never want to leave!

Cowgate – it's a "life's about living" kind of thing!

These days, young Bun, like the other lads, earns his bread on the right side of the law. In his case, he now works for a large printing firm. However, I would not be surprised if, after this here book, he got a bit of advertisement work for products such as Vick's hot lemon drinks or their vapour rub. Naturally, at least 50% of the proceeds would go to my and Durkin's accounts.

Jason "Popeye" Alison has a lucrative existence as a taxi driver. He will drive you and a friend round our fair city, 24/7, with handbrake turns thrown in at no extra cost. No change given, tips expected…

Then we have Master "Lights out in the second" Henton, who now kicks ass as a store manager with a large supermarket chain. I hear he has not only taken productivity through the roof, but also in the last ten years has single-handedly taken the art of loathing to remarkable new heights round at his mother's.

'And what about the flattest head in sunny Cowgate?' I hear you snapping with excitement. Well, all I know for certain is… he passed his driving test in 2002 and has not left his parents' home since.

The visual continues… Our egg-headed friend, young Ingram, is now working as a sales representative and buyer for a large sportswear manufacturer. Johnnie-boy has changed very little physically and he still has that unmistakeable cheeky grin and a razor-sharp wit. I expect his future role as an Easter egg stunt double is only a phone call away.

Durkin and I, who have obviously left our meagre jobs by now, owing to the global success of this book, are now living the life of Riley on an island just east of the Maldives. It goes without saying that Johnny Depp and Tom Cruise are the bookies' favourites to play us when the Blue Door hits the silver screen. Ha hey, this stuff is getting silly now.

I hear that these days, southern boy Wayne "I'm in tonight, mate" Aldred is doing quite well for himself down there in peaceful Huddersfield. That flyaway fringe remains and is central to our young buck's good looks, which explains his unique success with the opposite sex. Irresistible to men, women and cattle alike, Aldred earns his crust in the logistics industry. In his spare time, he is keen and active on the discotheque circuit within his native Yorkshire. He claims to have mastered the free-flowing Italian waltz by the age of eight. Taken into police custody, then released and re-arrested, for setting a dance floor alight during one of his fleeting performances, our Wayne, the running man, now chooses a quieter and more peaceful existence. Cheers, son, you're a total star!

We asked the lads for their input to this project and all seemed to agree. Everyone has different special memories. Popeye's all-time favourite is of asking me to have a sniff at a two-litre bottle of Coca Cabana, then squeezing the plastic bottle just as my nose was on the tip. I could smell nothing but passion fruit for days after getting bloody soaked and sticky from the force of the pop going up my nose and all over my hair and face.

He played a similar trick on me several months later. We were looking at the bargain shoe rack at Fenwick's department store, when he held up a pair of cheap Dunlop trainers and said, 'Look at the price of these.' As I put my head closer to the shoe, he smacked it full-belt into my face. I saw red and we ended up rolling around the "£5.99 or less" bargain bin.

John recalled Pops managing to squeeze through the smallest ever window of the dairy, (next to the Blue Door, as it happened), so that he could have a go on a milk float. Five minutes later, with the alarms going off, out came Popeye with two crates of pop and twenty-four yoghurts!

We recalled also the trips to the coast, when we dodged the Metro fare. If an inspector got on, we picked up tickets from the floor, pretending they were ours. We had to chew them first though, so he couldn't read them. How did we get away with it? Once, Pops pretended to be John, and Mrs Ingram was hit with a £10 fine . The family were actually on holiday in Majorca on the fateful day.

Wayne had memories of camping out in his mother's front garden and nicking milk off people's doorsteps. John and Neil were caught this one time, arrested and battered by their mothers while in the police station. Also, there was the game of Kill the Fox where, if you were caught you took a good old hiding. It was our version of Fox and Hounds. Our game was much less fun; we all took some serious beatings!

These pages record just a few of our experiences, growing up in Cowgate. Sadly, as we have recorded, the Blue Door and the dairy were pulled down in March 2007, to make way for a new supermarket development. However, the Blue Door will never disappear from our memories. Each of us nine young lads grasped life with both hands and turned it into an amazing roller-coaster ride for those few years. I want to thank you, boys, for some of the best times of my life.

Heading out fast again around the final bend, I can hear it. I can see it. Children's voices are again pulling me in. Tired old legs again at once become strong, as we run towards a great big door, painted blue. The Blue Door! Can you see it? It's mine… It's yours… It's ours…

For the ones who matter and for the greatest days of our lives, we give our thanks to

THE BLUE DOOR